Chess Choice
Challenge 2

Chris Ward

D1248690

B.T. Batsford Ltd, *London*

First published in 2002
© Chris Ward 2002

ISBN 07134 8705 4

British Library Cataloguing-in-Publication Data.
A catalogue record for this book is
available from the British Library.

Printed in Great Britain by
Creative Print and Design (Wales), Ebbw Vale
for the publishers,
B.T Batsford Ltd
64 Brewery Road
London N7 9NT

A member of the Chrysalis Group plc

Happy Birthday Deborah!

A BATSFORD CHESS BOOK

Preface

Just when you thought it was safe to go back in the water, *Chess Choice Challenge* has returned with even more bite than before!

Yes I promised that the questions in volume 2 would be even tougher and, well, although I'm not actually certain that they are, these thought-provokers are definitely a bit different.

Fun and learning are the order of the day here, i.e. for you to learn and for me to have fun in trying to tempt you into a wrong answer! Multiple choice questions at their most devious, it's A to E again. Maybe see you in *CCC3* and so until then take care.

Chris Ward

Beckenham, February 7th 2002

Contents

Introduction

So you couldn't resist joining me on another adventure heh? Didn't fancy missing out on all those nuggets of information that you might be able to pick up here in a vaguely entertaining sort of way?

Or perhaps you're a first timer? If so, the bottom line is that although I like to think that I'm a reasonable player, I've also had extensive experience in teaching chess at all levels. Able now to recognise common but incorrect modes of thinking, this style of quiz is perfect for helping to explain typical errors in thought patterns and adjusting them to the crystalline logic that is the truth!

Well whatever your reason, I'm obviously glad that you're here as every little purchase adds to my royalty cheque (or is that every purchase adds to my little royalty cheque?). Anyway I wasn't actually planning on droning on as we all know that some intros can drag and drag for no apparent reason.

Getting to the point, if you completed the first 'Chess Choice Challenge' then by now you should know the drill. The test format is multiple choice with 5 points being awarded to the correct answer. Occasionally though I may award 1, 2 or even 3 points for an alternative selection that I deem of reasonable value. Do be warned though: As their coach, I once lent the book to a member of the England ladies team who evidently had a good laugh reading some of the options. Later she informed me that she had 'even' got a few right. I had in fact hoped that she would in fact score quite highly and naturally enquired about what she had learnt about for example the endgames. I was none too impressed when her response involved confessing to not actually having looked at the positions!

Perhaps you can tell what the answer might be by the wording of a choice, but I wouldn't bank on it! I can be quite sneaky in that respect. Occasionally I include an obviously wrong answer but things aren't always as they may seem!

It's up to you how you do the puzzles. You may choose to read the book on a train or set the positions up and analyse them in your lounge with your favourite set and board. I would warn against using

'Fritz' or the like though as I have to confess that computer engines offer good advice without being duped by my red herrings! Basically that's cheating which in my book (this one in particular!) just isn't on. Of course if you can convince yourself that latest technology was merely confirming your own thoughts then that's fine!? It's your conscience after all!

There are four tests of twenty questions and marks therefore being out of 100, by all means check your results with the chart at the back of the book. However if I were you I would neither worry nor get too excited about how you are classified as it's merely an approximation based on a small sample.

I have tried to encompass a number of different themes throughout the course of the book and the questions have slightly less emphasis on the endgame than the last. As you will find though, that certainly doesn't make it easier! The answers are at the back and it was obviously my intention that these should educate. If you are not after detailed explanations then the 'Quick View' bit at the end also summarises points earned for each test (including bonuses).

I hope you enjoy reading it as much as I did writing it and having done my bit, now it's over to you...

Let's start with an easy one. How should White put to good use his space advantage?

A   1 ♘e6 is just the ticket.

B   1 ♗xf7+ is what the Doctor ordered.

C   1 ♗xh6 hits the mark.

D   1 ♘f5 is the best move.

E   It's clear that White has over-extended in the centre. The cautious 1 ♕f1 seeks to redress the balance.

A ☐ **B** ☐ **C** ☐ **D** ☐ **E** ☐ **Points**............

It's White to play. Can he defend this king and pawn endgame?

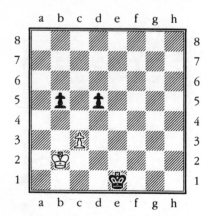

A   Yes but he must obtain the opposition with 1 ♔c1.

B   1 ♔a1 is the one correct defence.

C   White can do what he wants but with competent play Black will win.

D   Funnily enough the king can move to any DARK square to hold the draw.

E   Actually moving the king to any LIGHT square will bring success in the drawing department.

A ☐ **B** ☐ **C** ☐ **D** ☐ **E** ☐ **Points**............

With Black to play in this position, what is happening?

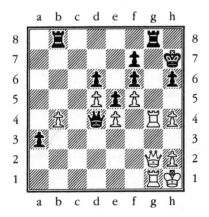

A   A drawish rook and pawn endgame is imminent.

B   Black will lose as he either gives up his queen or gets mated down the g-file.

C   The outwardly risky 1...♖gc8 will see Black through to victory.

D   Black will win because of some crafty play and his strong passed a-pawn.

E   With best play the game should end in a draw by perpetual check.

A ☐ **B** ☐ **C** ☐ **D** ☐ **E** ☐ **Points**............

Aside from repeating the position, what move would be the biggest indication that Black has the correct plan in mind to win this position?

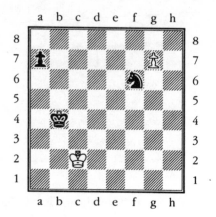

A   A mean question! However valiantly Black battles, correct White defence will lead to a draw.

B   1...♘g8.

C   1...♔c5.

D   1...a6.

E   1...a5.

A ☐ **B** ☐ **C** ☐ **D** ☐ **E** ☐ **Points**...........

A thematic break in isolated queen's pawn positions is d4-d5. Would 1 d5 be a good idea here?

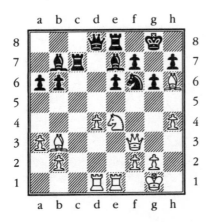

A   Yes it's an excellent move that would leave White clearly better.

B   No. 1...exd5 would be good for Black.

C   No. 1...♘xd5 avoids any tricks and leaves White worse.

D   No. 1...♗xd5 would ultimately leave Black a clear pawn up.

E   Well it's okay. However after 1...♘xe4 the resulting position is about equal.

A ☐ **B** ☐ **C** ☐ **D** ☐ **E** ☐ **Points**............

In the following position which of the following suggestions would NOT succeed in holding the draw?

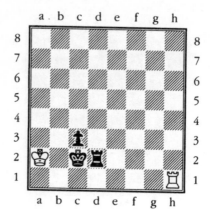

A   1 ♖h3

B   1 ♖h8

C   1 ♖g1

D   1 ♔a3

E   Beware the trick question! All of the above suggestions should lose.

A ☐ **B** ☐ **C** ☐ **D** ☐ **E** ☐ **Points**...........

Black has sacrificed material to reach this position. With White to play, what is now true?

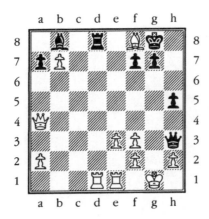

A   Black will win relatively quickly by force.

B   Black should win but unless White resigns prematurely, it will go to an endgame.

C   White can win by sacrificing his own queen with his next move.

D   Relatively simple play should see White to victory.

E   The game should end in a draw.

A ☐ **B** ☐ **C** ☐ **D** ☐ **E** ☐ **Points**............

Currently contemplating his 4th move, has Black already blundered?

A   A ridiculous question. There is nothing strange about this position!

B   Yes. It's as straightforward as it looks. The black bishop is trapped and his last move of 3...♗h5 was to say the least poor!

C   No but Black should avoid losing a piece with 4...♗g6 intending 5 f5 e6.

D   No provided Black plays the only serious possibility 4...e6.

E   No. He doesn't have to lose a piece although 4...e5!? looks promising.

A ☐   **B** ☐   **C** ☐   **D** ☐   **E** ☐   **Points**...........

Test One   Q9

How should White kick off the tough task of defending this tricky ending?

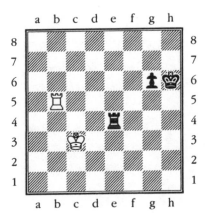

A   1 ♔d3.

B   1 ♖b1.

C   1 ♖b8.

D   1 ♖b6.

E   1 ♖a5.

A ☐ B ☐ C ☐ D ☐ E ☐ **Points**............

In the following position White seems to have got into a bit of a tangle. Objectively speaking, of the choices below what is his best chance?

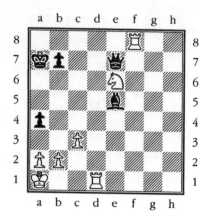

A   1 ♖dd8.

B   1 ♖fd8.

C   1 ♖f5.

D   1 ♖ff1.

E   There is no chance whatsoever.

A ☐ **B** ☐ **C** ☐ **D** ☐ **E** ☐ **Points**............

For his piece, White has obvious attacking chances. In this
position though, what is the most accurate way for him to proceed?

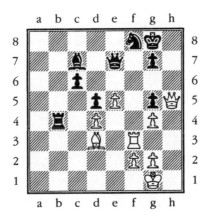

A   1 ♖f7.

B   1 ♖xf8+.

C   1 ♗g6.

D   1 ♖h3.

E   1 e6.

A ☐ B ☐ C ☐ D ☐ E ☐ **Points**...........

Currently a pawn down, Black is struggling in this position. What is his best practical attempt to get anything out of the game?

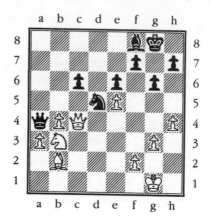

A   1...♝xb4.

B   1...♞xb4.

C   1...♛b5.

D   1...g5.

E   1...c5.

A ☐ B ☐ C ☐ D ☐ E ☐ **Points**...........

Both sides are attacking furiously in the following position. However it is Black to move. Does he have a big hit?

A Yes 1...♖xa2+ is crushing.

B Yes and 1...♛xc3 is just the move that he is looking for.

C Yes as 1...♞xe4 seeks to tear away the relevant defences.

D Not exactly. He must remain calm and 1...♝e8 offers the required support to his own kingside. The position is about equal.

E No. The fact is that White has a sturdy defence whereas the wall around his opponent's king is relatively flimsy. Black can patch things up in the very short run but he will ultimately struggle.

A ☐ **B** ☐ **C** ☐ **D** ☐ **E** ☐ **Points**............

Here is a rook ending that occurred in a real game. What is the most practical (and best!) move for Black to play?

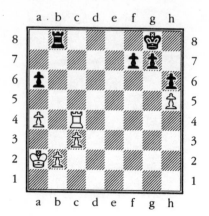

A   1...f5.

B   1...g5.

C   1...g6.

D   1...♜b6.

E   1...♜e8.

It certainly appears that White has a strong attack but how should he persevere?

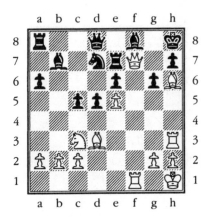

A   With 1 ♗g7+ of course!

B   With the stunning 1 ♕xg6.

C   With 1 ♕f4. White should come backwards in order to go forward.

D   With 1 ♕xf8+ leading to a superior endgame.

E   A not mentioned above solid move possibly accompanied with a draw offer would be more appropriate as with the attack rebuffed, the tide is turning in Black's favour.

A ☐ **B** ☐ **C** ☐ **D** ☐ **E** ☐ **Points**............

It's White to play in the following endgame. Paying close attention to the wording, which of the following statements is true?

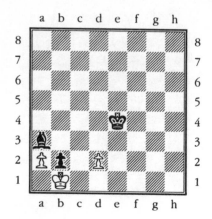

A   White is lost whatever he plays.

B   Thanks in the main to stalemate tricks, any move here will lead to a draw.

C   1 ♔c2 is the only move that will LOSE White the game.

D   1 d3+ is the only move that will DRAW White the game.

E   1 d4 is the only move that will DRAW White the game.

A ☐ **B** ☐ **C** ☐ **D** ☐ **E** ☐ **Points**............

In a recent encounter between two strong players, Black continued in the following position with 1...♛xc1. What is your view of this temporary queen sacrifice?

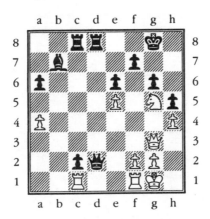

A   It was completely unnecessary and Black will suffer as a result of his cockiness.

B   It is a stylish way to help terminate an obviously good position.

C   Black will emerge with a slight endgame advantage but he has better moves here.

D   Facing a dangerous queen and knight pairing, it was the easiest way to bale out to a level position.

E   It's all rather unclear!

A ☐   **B** ☐   **C** ☐   **D** ☐   **E** ☐   **Points**...........

With White to play in this interesting knight ending, what's happening?

A   White should play 1 ♔c3 when the game should be a draw.

B   After 1 h5 White is winning.

C   After 1 f5 White is winning.

D   After 1 ♘xh7 White is winning.

E   Whatever White does Black stands better.

A ☐ **B** ☐ **C** ☐ **D** ☐ **E** ☐ **Points**...........

Considering a 5th move for Black, what would be acceptable at Grandmaster level? Make the most appropriate selection out of the choices below.

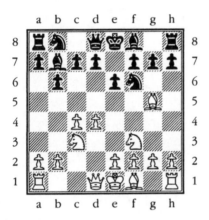

A   5...d5 or 5...c5 but not 5...h6.

B   5...♝b4 or 5...♝xf3 but not 5...♝e7.

C   5...♝e7 or 5...d5 but not 5...c5.

D   5...h6 or 5...♝e7 but not 5...♝b4.

E   5...♝b4 or 5...♝e7 but not 5...d5.

A ☐ **B** ☐ **C** ☐ **D** ☐ **E** ☐ **Points**...........

It's White to play with little left on the board. What's going down?

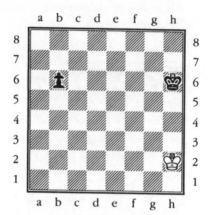

A   His position! He's lost because his king is outside the square of the enemy pawn that will successfully promote in 5 moves time.

B   White can draw but only if he starts with 1 ♔g3.

C   White can draw but only if he starts with 1 ♔g2.

D   White can draw but only if he starts with 1 ♔g1.

E   White could stop the pawn in a straight race but Black is winning because he will be able to obtain the opposition.

A ☐ **B** ☐ **C** ☐ **D** ☐ **E** ☐ **Points**............

White was considering a 21st move of 21 dxc6 leading to the position below. Assuming that there was an alternative available that would have lead to equality, would it be a wise choice?

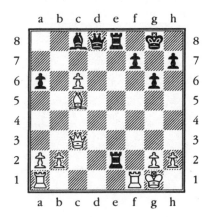

A   No as 21...♖xg2+ is crushing.

B   No as 21...♗h3 is strong for Black.

C   No because of the simple 21...♕d5.

D   No as the variation 21...♕g5 22 ♖f2 ♗h3 is very convincing for Black.

E   Yes actually it looks rather good for White.

A ☐ **B** ☐ **C** ☐ **D** ☐ **E** ☐   **Points**............

It's tactics time! Which of the following sacrifices will work in this position? Note that there may (but not necessarily!) be more than one correct answer.

A   1 ♘xg6.

B   1 ♗xg6.

C   1 ♘xf7.

D   1 ♖xf7.

E   1 ♕xh7+.

A □ B □ C □ D □ E □ **Points**............

Is White, to play, in a hopeless situation here?

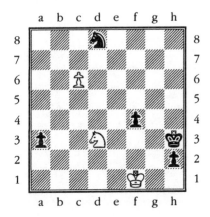

A   Certainly not. Via 1 ♘f2+ and 2 c7 next he is actually winning.

B   Beginning with 1 ♘f2+ White can draw with some clever play to follow.

C   Provided 1 ♘xf4+ is played White can hold the draw.

D   A devious stalemate idea comes into play in a forcing variation. White can draw.

E   'Hopeless' is a strong word but although it would be premature to resign here and now, with accurate play Black will win.

A ☐ **B** ☐ **C** ☐ **D** ☐ **E** ☐ **Points**............

Black has sacrificed plenty of material to reach the following position. Clearly accuracy is required. What is his best move?

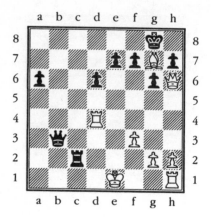

A   1...♜xg2.

B   1...f6.

C   1...♛b1+.

D   1...♛e6+.

E   1...♛c3+.

A ☐ B ☐ C ☐ D ☐ E ☐ **Points**............

Having previously sacrificed a pawn, what is White's best move in this position?

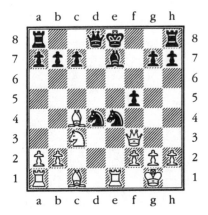

A   1 ♘xe4.

B   1 ♕f4.

C   1 ♕h3.

D   1 ♕d1.

E   1 ♕h5+.

A ☐ B ☐ C ☐ D ☐ E ☐ **Points**............

White has sacrificed a pawn but appears to have some reasonable attacking chances. Take your pick of the moves below to make a good suggestion to Black.

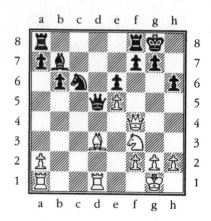

A   The intriguing 1...♞d4.

B   The counter-attacking 1...g5.

C   The solid 1...♜ad8.

D   The also rook-developing 1...♜ac8.

E   The cautious 1...♛a5.

A ☐ **B** ☐ **C** ☐ **D** ☐ **E** ☐ **Points**............

White's active pieces appear to offer some compensation for his potentially weak isolated queen's pawn. How might he strive to take advantage of his opponent's back rank pieces and vulnerable queen?

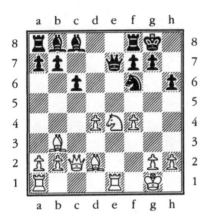

A   With the exposing 1 ♘g5.

B   With the queen deflecting 1 ♗b4.

C   With the centre blasting 1 d5.

D   With the queenside pressurising 1 ♘c5.

E   With the edging forward 1 ♕c5.

A ☐ B ☐ C ☐ D ☐ E ☐ **Points**............

Concerning this tough bishop ending with White to play, which of the statements below is true?

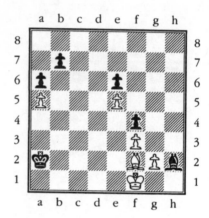

A   White should play 1 ♗g1 after which he is winning.

B   White should play 1 g4 after which he is winning.

C   White should play 1 ♔e2 after which he is winning.

D   The game should end in a draw.

E   Black is winning.

A ☐   **B** ☐   **C** ☐   **D** ☐   **E** ☐   **Points**............

Despite being a rook (for a couple of pawns) down, Black has some obvious threats. Is there any way for White to save (i.e. draw or win) the day?

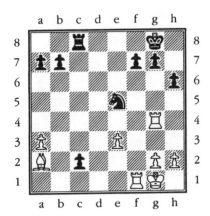

A   No. With reasonable play Black will win.

B   Yes but only starting with 1 ♗xf7+.

C   Yes but only starting with 1 ♖xf7.

D   Yes but only starting with 1 ♖gf4.

E   Yes but starting with a move not suggested in B, C or D.

A ☐ **B** ☐ **C** ☐ **D** ☐ **E** ☐ **Points**............

Which of the following statements is the closest to the truth about the following position in which it is White to move?

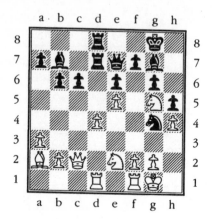

A   1 ♘f4 is White's best move when he stands better.

B   1 ♘xe6 would destroy Black's position.

C   1 ♘e4 leaves White with a simple edge.

D   A different White move (to the ones suggested above) would leave White close to winning.

E   The reality is that White has some initiative on the kingside but Black has pressure against d4. With all things taken into consideration the position is fairly equal.

A ☐ **B** ☐ **C** ☐ **D** ☐ **E** ☐ **Points**............

It's Black to play in the so clearly staged following position. What on earth is going on?

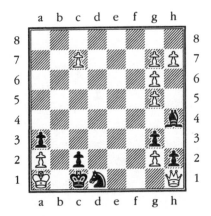

A   After promoting to as many queens as he needs White will win.

B   Black wins after 1...♗xg5.

C   It's a draw thanks to some sneaky stalemate ideas.

D   White wins provided he is careful.

E   What sort of question is this anyway? I want my money back!

A ☐ **B** ☐ **C** ☐ **D** ☐ **E** ☐ **Points**............

Here Black, to play, has three pawns for the exchange but a couple of them look like dropping off. What is his best practical chance for a win?

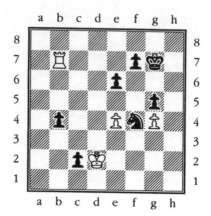

A   1...♘e2.

B   1...♘d3.

C   1...b3.

D   1...c1=♕+.

E   1...♚f6.

A ☐ B ☐ C ☐ D ☐ E ☐ **Points**............

With Black's bishop locked out of the game on a7, there is the odd interesting continuation. Should White to move be tempted by a sacrifice?

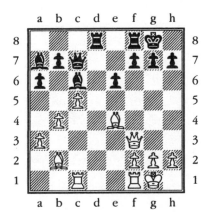

A   Yes 1 ♗xg7 should be curtains for Black.

B   Yes 1 ♗xh7+ is a standard idea.

C   Not just yet. He should build up slowly with 1 ♖c4.

D   No. 1 ♗xc6 gives Black a lasting weakness when White should concentrate his efforts on the queenside.

E   No. 1 ♖fe1 is a sensible multi-purpose move.

A ☐ **B** ☐ **C** ☐ **D** ☐ **E** ☐ **Points**............

Contemplating his 30ᵗʰ move, being two pawns down and having to deal with the threat of 31 ♖h4+, Black chose to resign. Was this such a dreadful decision?

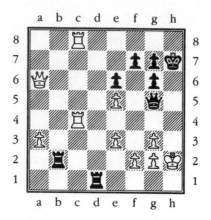

A Well not really as he is losing anyway.

B Absolutely as he is actually winning the game.

C Yes as a clever sequence can see him force a draw by perpetual check.

D Yes as he can achieve a very drawish rook and pawn endgame.

E Well, you win some, you lose some and basically I don't really know!

A ☐ **B** ☐ **C** ☐ **D** ☐ **E** ☐ **Points**............

Can Black, to play, defend this deceptively simple-looking king and pawn endgame?

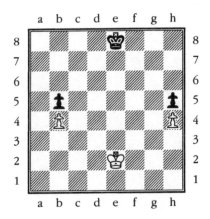

A   Defend, what do you mean defend? He is the one that is winning!

B   Yes but only with 1...♚e7.

C   Yes but only with 1...♚d8.

D   Surprisingly any first move will do and he can still draw.

E   No. With accurate play White will win.

A ☐ **B** ☐ **C** ☐ **D** ☐ **E** ☐ **Points**............

16 moves into the game which has reached a typical 'Hedgehog' style middlegame, can you suggest a suitable move for Black?

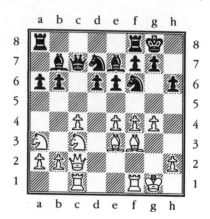

A   16...d5.

B   16...b5.

C   16...♘h7.

D   16...♖fe8.

E   16...♖ac8.

A ☐ **B** ☐ **C** ☐ **D** ☐ **E** ☐ **Points**...........

White has three connected passed pawns but his rook appears to be in a spot of bother. How should he play and what is the most likely outcome?

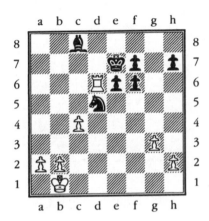

A   1 ♖xd5 is best with a probable White win.

B   1 ♖c6 is best as it leads to a winning king and pawn endgame.

C   1 c5 is a trivial White win.

D   Each of the above three suggestions are of approximately equal value with a draw being on the cards.

E   Whatever White chooses he is lost.

A ☐ **B** ☐ **C** ☐ **D** ☐ **E** ☐ **Points**............

It's White to play here. What's happening?

A   He must play 1 ♔f1 when he will achieve a draw.

B   He must play 1 ♔h1 in order to obtain the draw.

C   Either 1 ♔f1 or 1 ♔h1 are sufficient. Careful play thereafter will guarantee half a point.

D   Whatever he does White is lost.

E   The position is deceptive. In fact Black is the one in trouble!

A ☐ **B** ☐ **C** ☐ **D** ☐ **E** ☐ **Points**............

Just six moves into the game, having arrived at some sort of Queen's Gambit Accepted position, Black seems to be clinging on to his extra c-pawn. How should White set about dealing with this situation?

A   By undermining the b-pawn with 7 a4.

B   By hitting it directly with 7 b3.

C   Actually the tactic 7 ♘xb5 seems to work.

D   White should ignore the queenside and concentrate on the centre. 7 e4 is best.

E   The simplest is to continue with the development on the kingside. 7 g3 is sensible.

A ☐ **B** ☐ **C** ☐ **D** ☐ **E** ☐ **Points**............

Under time pressure to reach the time control at move 40 I once bashed out 39 c5-c6 leading to the following position. Was this a completely dumb idea?

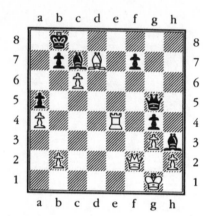

A   Well it's not a very wise practical decision but there should be no serious problems (White is still winning).

B   Yes, Black will now be able to force a draw by perpetual check.

C   Yes it's a disaster as Black can now win pretty much by force.

D   Yes as now a massive stalemate idea comes into play.

E   Not really. The position was equal before and it still is!

A ☐ **B** ☐ **C** ☐ **D** ☐ **E** ☐ **Points**............

It's Black to play in this interesting endgame. What's happening?

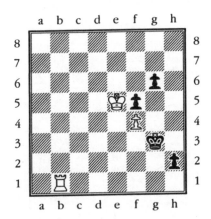

A   After 1...♚g2 Black is winning.

B   Black must play 1...♚g2 in order to draw.

C   Black should play 1...♚g4 and will draw.

D   Black should play 1...♚f3 and will draw.

E   White is winning.

A ☐ **B** ☐ **C** ☐ **D** ☐ **E** ☐ **Points**............

White has open lines where a couple of his pawns once were. What is the best way for him to continue his attack?

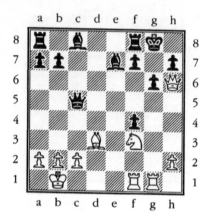

A   1 h4.

B   1 ♘g5.

C   1 ♖g5.

D   1 ♗xg6.

E   1 ♖xg6+.

A ☐ B ☐ C ☐ D ☐ E ☐ **Points**............

With Black to play here, how would you assess this position?

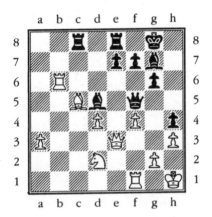

A   White is a clear pawn up and should really win.

B   Taking everything into consideration, White is slightly better.

C   Black's bishop pair offers him just about enough compensation for the pawn. The chances are equal.

D   Black is completely winning.

E   No doubt most texts would annotate this as 'unclear'!

A ☐ **B** ☐ **C** ☐ **D** ☐ **E** ☐ **Points**............

White has just played 33 ♕(e2)xa6. What's the truth about this ending?

A   Black must really play 33...♕c4 when he's slightly worse but has good drawing chances.

B   Black should play 33...♕c4 when he has good winning chances in the ensuing rook and pawn ending.

C   It is vital to retain a material balance and there is nothing clearly good for White after the best move 33...♕xb2.

D   Black can't afford to hang around. Passed pawns are made to be pushed and 33...e5 is correct.

E   Before any serious action is taken, the black king should head for safety. 33...♔f8 aims for the shelter of the kingside.

A ☐ **B** ☐ **C** ☐ **D** ☐ **E** ☐ **Points**............

It's White to play in this crazy position. What is going on?

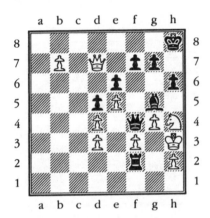

A   White can obtain a favourable endgame.

B   White is winning relatively quickly by force.

C   The game should end quickly in a draw.

D   Black can obtain a favourable endgame.

E   Black is winning relatively quickly by force.

A ☐   **B** ☐   **C** ☐   **D** ☐   **E** ☐   **Points**............

What's happening in this tense middlegame struggle in which it is White to move?

A   White should play 1 exf6 which is clearly better.

B   White should play 1 ♗xf6 which is clearly better.

C   White has neglected his queenside development and should play 1 ♘bd2 with equal chances.

D   White has neglected his queenside development but should play 1 ♗h4 with equal chances.

E   It's probably fair to say that Black has a slight edge.

A ☐ **B** ☐ **C** ☐ **D** ☐ **E** ☐ **Points**...........

Nine moves into the game, should White, to play, venture into taking the black pawn on b7?

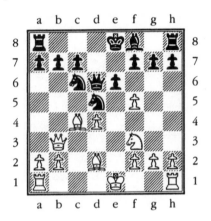

A   Objectively yes, as White is worse and 10 ♕xb7 should lead to a draw by repetition.

B   Yes. There is nothing that clear for Black and a pawn is a pawn.

C   No. It is a poisoned pawn and White will lose material by force.

D   No. Although it doesn't instantly lose, Black will have plenty of long-term pressure.

E   No. Taking the pawn is unclear but White has at least one better alternative.

A ☐   **B** ☐   **C** ☐   **D** ☐   **E** ☐   **Points**...........

Get your counting hat on! Where should White to play move?

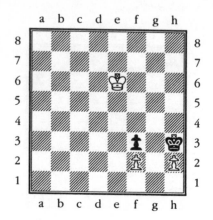

A   1 ♔d6.

B   1 ♔d5.

C   1 ♔e5.

D   1 ♔f5.

E   It doesn't matter. Black is winning whatever White does!

A ☐ **B** ☐ **C** ☐ **D** ☐ **E** ☐ **Points**............

Black is contemplating the move 21...♘c3+ in the following position. Which of the statements below holds the most truth?

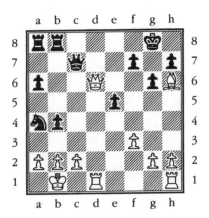

A   It wins by force.

B   As Black is worse otherwise, it is a good way to effectively force a draw.

C   Alas it's a nice idea but it simply doesn't work and with careful defence White would win.

D   21...♛xd6 is a better move leading to an equal ending.

E   It's too difficult for humans to calculate and this sort of position is best left for computers!

A ☐ **B** ☐ **C** ☐ **D** ☐ **E** ☐ **Points**............

The following position is not as trivial as it may look (or is it?). Bearing that in mind, with White to play what's going on?

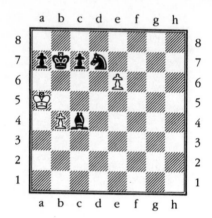

A   After 1 e7 White will win.

B   After 1 b5 a draw is likely.

C   1 exd7 is best when White will win.

D   1 exd7 is best when White can hold the draw thanks to an important stalemate idea.

E   1 exd7 is best but Black can still hold the draw.

A ☐ **B** ☐ **C** ☐ **D** ☐ **E** ☐ **Points**............

White, to move, clearly has an attractive position but of the choices below which is his strongest continuation?

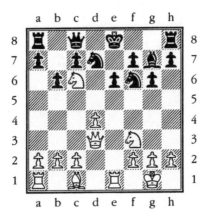

A   1 h4.

B   1 ♘fe5.

C   1 ♕a3.

D   1 ♘g5.

E   1 d5.

A ☐ B ☐ C ☐ D ☐ E ☐ **Points**............

Assuming (as always) best play, of the explanations below what best details how this bishop ending should turn out?

A White should carefully edge forward and win with little trouble.

B Bishop and rook's and bishop's pawns vs bishop (provided the pawns aren't too far advanced) is a well known draw.

C The position is a draw but only because the rook's pawn promotes on the opposite colour to the remaining bishop.

D The endgame is drawn now because the pawns have been advanced too soon.

E Black will be able to claim a draw by the '50 move rule' before White gets the opportunity to promote a pawn.

A ☐ **B** ☐ **C** ☐ **D** ☐ **E** ☐ **Points**...........

Test Three

What is true about the following position in which it is Black to play?

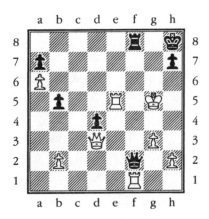

A   1...h6+ is the best move.

B   Black should play 1...♖g8+ in order to draw.

C   Black should play 1...♖g8+ after which he is winning.

D   After 1...♛xf1 White must trade queens when the rook ending should be drawn.

E   Black has a really strong move, which is not mentioned above.

A ☐ **B** ☐ **C** ☐ **D** ☐ **E** ☐ **Points**...........

White has just played 15 h3 leading to the following position. Which of the statements below most accurately describe the options available to Black?

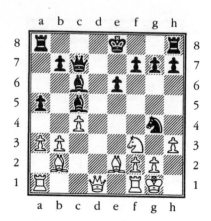

A   15...♘xf2 is strong and 11...♖d8 is good too.

B   15...♕g3 is best and 11...h5 is attractive too.

C   15...♗xf3 is practically winning and 11...♖d8 is also very powerful.

D   15...h5 looks promising although 11...♗xf3 is also very reasonable.

E   15...♘f6 is the most sensible move with 11...♘h6 also playable.

| A ☐ | B ☐ | C ☐ | D ☐ | E ☐ | **Points**............ |

Black is the exchange up but can you suggest a winning plan in this slightly awkward looking situation?

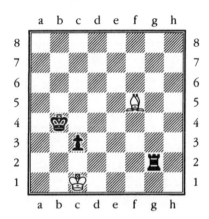

A   Yes it's very straightforward. 1...♚b3 will suffice, with a back rank check next wrapping things up nicely.

B   Yes but he must sacrifice his pawn with a timely ...c2.

C   Yes but he must leave the pawn where it stands in order to hunt down the bishop with his king and rook.

D   Yes but it will involve an under-promotion.

E   I'm afraid not. Provided White defends sensibly he will hold the draw.

A ☐ **B** ☐ **C** ☐ **D** ☐ **E** ☐ **Points**............

White has just played 30 ♖ae1. Take some time out to study this lively middlegame and decide on which of the suggestions below you think is Black's best.

A   30...♕a8.

B   30...♖c8.

C   30...♖xf2.

D   30...exd3.

E   30...e3.

A ☐ **B** ☐ **C** ☐ **D** ☐ **E** ☐ **Points**............

White has just played 32 ♗(c4)-b5 (which may be a mistake!?).
Regarding the move 32...♖b8, should Black now exploit the b-file
pin in this manner?

A No as it loses to both 33 d7 and 33 ♗xc6.

B No as it loses to 33 ♗xf6+.

C Yes as he will win at least the exchange and then convert the
resulting endgame.

D Yes as he can draw either the opposite or same coloured
bishop ending that will most likely result.

E Strictly speaking, none of the above are accurate.

A ☐ **B** ☐ **C** ☐ **D** ☐ **E** ☐ **Points**............

What is the truth about this tricky king and pawn ending in which it is White to play?

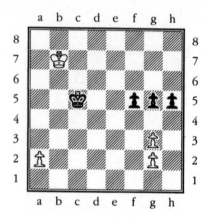

A   White ought to play 1 a4 when he should go on to win.

B   1 a4 is best when White can draw.

C   1 a3 is the best move.

D   1 ♔c7 is the best move.

E   Black is winning.

A ☐ **B** ☐ **C** ☐ **D** ☐ **E** ☐ **Points**...........

Black has two more centre pawns than his opponent but White has just played the dangerous-looking 15 h5. After taking some time to study the position, can you conclude whether Black is really in trouble?

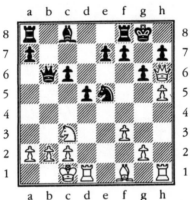

A   Yes, White's basic h-pawn attack will lead to mate.

B   Yes. Black can defend against the mate but only at the cost of significant material.

C   No. White's attack can be easily rebuffed leaving Black pretty much a pawn up for nothing.

D   It's not about material. Black's attack hits home before White's.

E   It's a complex position and with all things taken into consideration there are approximately equal chances for both sides!

A ☐ B ☐ C ☐ D ☐ E ☐ **Points**............

With reference to this endgame in which it is White to play, can you identify the correct statement amongst the false ones below?

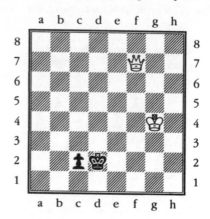

A   Wherever the attacker's king, a queen (whose side it is to move) always defeats a pawn on the 7th rank.

B   If the 7th rank pawn is on the rook's or bishop's file and the king up with the pawn (as above), it's a draw provided the attacking king is (as above) a sufficient distance away.

C   Black will be able to draw this position provided at the critical moment he under-promotes.

D   Black will be able to draw this position provided he is prepared to rest his king on a1.

E   Some ♔+♕ vs ♔+♙ endings are drawn and some are won. The above example is of the latter variety.

A ☐   B ☐   C ☐   D ☐   E ☐   **Points**............

Okay, so the following position just may have been contrived! White has a winning combination (it's a long one!) and all you have to do is determine the move at the end of the sequence that finally sounds the death knell. So which of the choices below will it be?

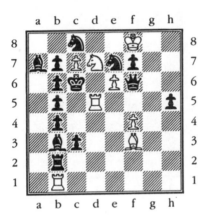

A ♖xf6.

B e8=♘+.

C ♕a8+.

D ♖a1+.

E None of the above. Under close scrutiny it later came to light that the famous composers of this study had erred in its creation and in fact the best that White can do is draw.

A ☐ B ☐ C ☐ D ☐ E ☐ **Points**............

You would expect to be able to win when a bishop for a pawn up, but regarding the ending below, with White to play, could this be one of those exceptions?

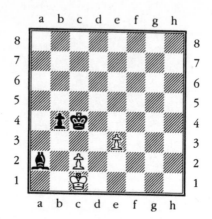

A   Yes, White draws with 1 ♔b2.

B   Yes, White draws with 1 ♔d2.

C   Yes, White draws with 1 ♔d1.

D   Yes, White draws with 1 e4.

E   Alas not. Black is winning.

A ☐ B ☐ C ☐ D ☐ E ☐ Points............

This should be like a walk in the park for you now! With White to play, what really gets to the crux of the matter?

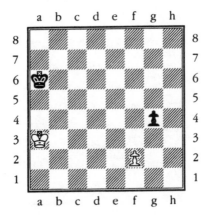

A   Via 1 ♔b4 White will win.

B   Via 1 ♔a2 White will win.

C   Via 1 ♔a4 White will win.

D   Admittedly 1 ♔a4 is probably White's best practical try but it's a draw anyhow.

E   Black is winning.

A ☐ **B** ☐ **C** ☐ **D** ☐ **E** ☐ **Points**............

Test Four

White has sacrificed the exchange and a pawn to reach the following position. Contemplating his 29th move, how should White continue?

A   29 ♖xf7.

B   29 ♔c2.

C   29 ♗g3+.

D   29 ♖f6+.

E   29 ♖f5.

A ☐ B ☐ C ☐ D ☐ E ☐ Points...........

White has just played 56 g5 to reach the following position in a game between two strong players. Evidently considering his position hopeless, Black opted to resign. Was this a poor decision?

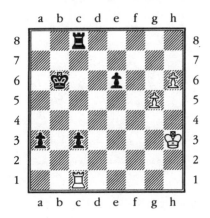

A   Not really. He could have played on a few more moves but in situations such as this, connected pawns are usually far superior to isolated ones.

B   'Poor' is somewhat of an under-statement as he is actually winning due in main to the fact that his passed pawns are further advanced than his opponent's.

C   Definitely. A rather clever but at the same time quite simple idea offers an excellent drawing defence.

D   As the worst that you can ever do is lose, there is never any point in resigning anyway!

E   Not if he had to be home in time for tea!

A ☐ **B** ☐ **C** ☐ **D** ☐ **E** ☐ **Points**...........

What is true of the following ending?

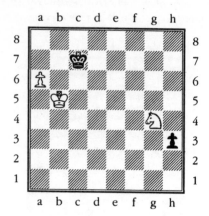

A   White is winning whoever is to move.

B   It's a draw whoever is to move.

C   Black is winning whoever is to move.

D   If it's White to move he is winning but if it's Black to move it's a draw.

E   If it's Black to move White is winning but if it's White to move it's a draw.

A ☐ **B** ☐ **C** ☐ **D** ☐ **E** ☐ **Points**...........

It's Black to play in this rook and pawn ending. Possibly referring to your hopefully now fairly extensive memory endgame database, what's your assessment of this one?

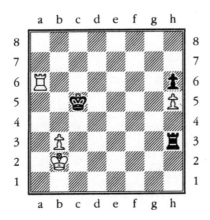

A   White will be able to take on h6, play ♖h8 and advance his pawn to h7 and Bob's your uncle! (White wins comfortably).

B   White will win the pawn on h6 but the winning plan is not as detailed in A. There will be a little fidgeting but the first player will emerge victorious.

C   It's a draw because all rook and pawn endings are drawn!

D   Black will be able to hold the queen vs rook ending that will soon appear.

E   Black has a tactic to more or less force the draw.

A ☐ **B** ☐ **C** ☐ **D** ☐ **E** ☐ **Points**...........

Regarding the following position in which it is Black to play, there are some seriously tempting possibilities given below. Which do you think is the best?

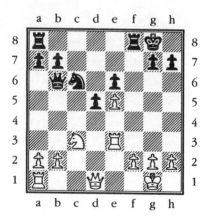

A   1...♛xb2.

B   1...d4.

C   1...♞xe5.

D   1...♜xf2.

E   1...g5.

A ☐ **B** ☐ **C** ☐ **D** ☐ **E** ☐ **Points**............

Here the knight looks pretty poorly placed but, on the move, do you think that White has any serious chance of ultimately conceding it in order to achieve a draw?

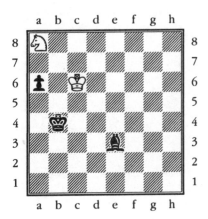

A   No. Knights are notoriously bad at stopping passed rook's pawns and with Black having a bishop as well, this is no exception.

B   Yes but only if he starts with 1 ♘b6.

C   Yes but only if he starts with 1 ♘c7.

D   Yes but only if he selects 1 ♔d5.

E   This is a famous position and White can draw in a slightly unusual way with a first move not mentioned above.

A ☐   **B** ☐   **C** ☐   **D** ☐   **E** ☐   **Points**............

Test Four

Which of the statements below is true about this king and pawn ending in which it is White to move.

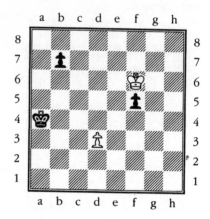

A   Black is winning.

B   White should draw with 1 ♔xf5.

C   White should draw with 1 ♔e5.

D   White should draw with 1 d4.

E   White should draw with a starting move not mentioned above.

A ☐ **B** ☐ **C** ☐ **D** ☐ **E** ☐ **Points**...........

Making an assessment of this complex middlegame position in which it is White to play, which of the following summaries come closest to satisfying you.

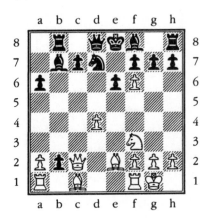

A   13 ♛xb2 looks fairly promising for White.

B   13 ♝xb2 is probably best but after say 13...♞xf6, it is questionable as to whether White has enough for the pawn.

C   13 ♞e5 is a stunner. It's practically game, set and match!

D   White should play 13 fxg7 which would lead to a crazy position that clearly favours him.

E   White should play 13 fxg7 leading to a position of equal chances.

A ☐ **B** ☐ **C** ☐ **D** ☐ **E** ☐ **Points**............

It's White to play in the following endgame. Should he expect to win this position?

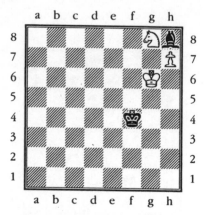

A   No as the bishop will always be able to give itself up for the pawn.

B   No. Actually he will be able to win the bishop but it will involve his king being trapped in the corner in an exceptional position where a king, knight and a pawn can only draw against a bare king.

C   Yes and actually it's all rather trivial with Black probably resigning in 4 or 5 moves time.

D   Yes but it will take a fair bit of manoeuvring (and a fair few moves).

E   Well he can expect what he wants but it's a game of two halves that can go either way!

A ☐ B ☐ C ☐ D ☐ E ☐ Points...........

In this middlegame, Black had the interesting candidate move 25...♛f3 amongst his options. After making some investigations, what do you think of it?

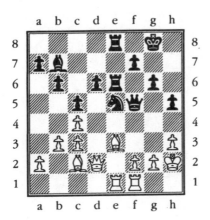

A It certainly is interesting and concluding the game in a fair manner, the outcome should be a draw.

B It's beautiful. Black is winning.

C It's okay but the real deal is 25...♛xh3+.

D It's ridiculous and Black should prefer 25...♝e4.

E Whether or not it is good is irrelevant as 25...♞f3+ is a far easier win.

A ☐ **B** ☐ **C** ☐ **D** ☐ **E** ☐ **Points**............

Which of the suggestions below would be the wisest choice for White in this practical ending?

A   1 ♘f3.

B   1 ♘xf5.

C   1 ♘xg6.

D   1 ♘xa5.

E   1 ♘xc5.

A ☐ B ☐ C ☐ D ☐ E ☐ **Points**............

What on earth is going on in this crazy-looking endgame?

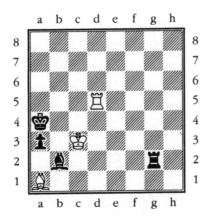

A   White can sacrifice his bishop in order to obtain a draw.

B   In a few moves the position should get down to king and rook vs king and rook i.e. a draw!

C   Black will reach a won rook and pawn vs rook ending.

D   Black will reach a won rook and knight vs rook situation.

E   A drawn rook and knight vs rook scenario should be reached.

A ☐ B ☐ C ☐ D ☐ E ☐ **Points**...........

Below is a hypothetical variation from a high-profile game. With White to play here, what should happen?

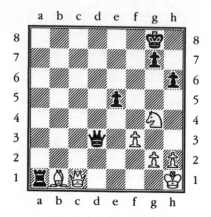

A   The arbiter should step in as the position is illegal.

B   White is winning.

C   It's a draw.

D   Black is winning.

E   None of the above!

A ☐   B ☐   C ☐   D ☐   E ☐   **Points**............

It's Black to play in the position below. What's going on?

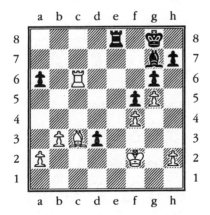

A   The inevitable rook and pawn ending will be slightly better for Black.

B   The inevitable rook and pawn ending will be slightly better for White.

C   Black is winning.

D   White is winning.

E   It is a relatively straightforward draw.

A ☐ **B** ☐ **C** ☐ **D** ☐ **E** ☐   **Points**............

Here White has just played 6 b2-b4 in an attempt to exploit the vulnerability of the offside knight. Is Black in trouble?

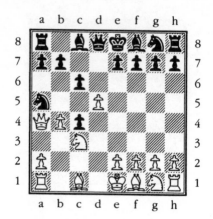

A   Definitely. He is losing a piece for practically nothing.

B   No because after 6...cxb3 7 axb3 he has 7...b6.

C   No because after 6...cxb3 7 axb3 he has 7...e6.

D   It's quite possible that he is worse but he is still in the game after 6...b5.

E   No because White has broken an opening principle by bringing his queen out early!

A ☐   **B** ☐   **C** ☐   **D** ☐   **E** ☐   **Points**...........

Twenty moves into an exciting game, instead of the obvious 21 ♘xg5, do you think that White can get away with the Greek gift style 21 ♗xh7+?

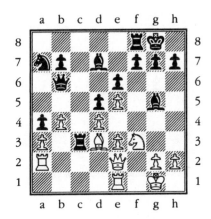

A   Yes and it's a very strong move!

B   Alas not in view of 21...♔h8.

C   Alas not in view of 21...♔xh7 22 ♘xg5+ ♔g8.

D   Alas not in view of 21...♔xh7 22 ♘xg5+ ♔h6.

E   Alas not in view of 21...♔xh7 22 ♘xg5+ ♔g6.

A ☐ **B** ☐ **C** ☐ **D** ☐ **E** ☐ **Points**............

It's Black to play in the following king and pawn ending. Can he draw it?

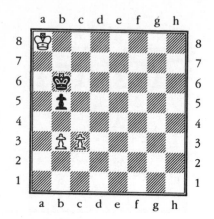

A   Yes so long as he starts with 1...♔a5.

B   Yes so long as he starts with 1...♔a6.

C   Yes so long as he starts with 1...♔c6.

D   Yes so long as he starts with 1...b4.

E   No, not if White plays accurately.

A ☐ **B** ☐ **C** ☐ **D** ☐ **E** ☐ **Points**............

Test One: Answers

Q1

Unbelievably this position was reached in a game played in the 2001 World U-10 championships! Whilst E is a complete load of twaddle, 1 ♘f5 is obviously a sensible-looking move (1 point for D). However full marks go to **C**. After 1 ♗xf7+ ♔xf7 Sebastian Pozzo from England continued with the extremely visual 2 ♘e6!!.

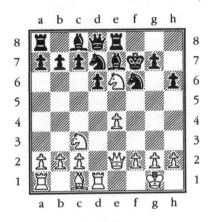

Due to Black's cramped circumstances he finds his queen smothered by his own pieces. The finish was beautiful: 2...♔xe6 3 ♕c4+ d5 4 ♘xd5 ♔f7 5 ♘f4+ ♔f8 6 ♘g6 mate.

Q2

Checking out some variations we have:

a) 1 ♔c2 ♔e2 when the white king is soon squeezed out, e.g. 2 ♔b2 ♔d2 3 ♔b3 ♔c1 4 ♔a3 ♔c2 5 ♔b4 ♔b2 6 ♔xb5 ♔xc3 and the d-pawn promotes.

b) 1 ♔c1 ♔e2 2 ♔c2 ♔e3. Alas, now White is deprived the chance of maintaining 'the opposition' with 3 ♔c3 as that square is already occupied by a pawn. Hence, say 3 ♔b2 ♔d2 4 ♔b3 ♔c1 with the same story as above. However:

c) 1 ♔a1!

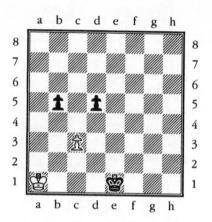

illustrated above is very crafty. White obtains the distant opposition. Now 1...b4 is met by 2 ♔b2 with the intention of taking the pawn next time when in the ensuing pawn pushes, Black wouldn't promote with check. The main point though is that 1...♔d1 can be met by 2 ♔b1, 1...♔d2 with 2 ♔b2 and 1...♔e2 with 2 ♔a2. All clever stuff and you will observe that, say in the latter instance, 2...♔d3 3 ♔b3 ♔d2 4 ♔b2 sees Black making no progress.

B gets the full 5 points and nothing for poor imitations!

Q3

Correct play should be 1...♕xg1+ (Not 1...♖gc8?? 2 ♖g7+ ♔h8 3 ♖h7+ ♔xh7 4 ♕g7 mate.) 2 ♕xg1 (rather than 2 ♔xg1? ♖xg4 3 ♕xg4+ a2 4 ♕d1 ♖xb4 with ...♖b1 up next) 2...♖xg4 (Black mustn't get too carried away e.g. 2...a2? 3 ♖xg8 ♖xg8 4 ♕a1 ♖a8 5 b5 with an easy White win.) 3 ♕xg4 a2 4 ♕g1! (much better than 4 ♕d1 which as above offers no defence to 4...♖xb4) 4...♖xb4 5 ♕a7 ♖b1+ 6 ♔g2 a1=♕ 7 ♕xf7+ ♔h8 8 ♕f8+ and a perpetual.

This accurate analysis was obviously done by both players in the recent game Kreiman-Christainsen, US Championship 2002, as they agreed a draw a short way into this sequence.

For 5 points **E** is spot on.

Q4

This is another fascinating one and beautiful in its simplicity. Via **B** (5 points) Black can make the most of his remaining pieces. First note that after 1...a5 2 ♔b2 a4 3 ♔a2 a3 4 ♔a1 ♔b3 5 ♔b1 there is no way for Black to win as, shackled by the g-pawn, the knight cannot get involved in the real action.

On the other hand a different plan entirely is 1...♘g8 2 ♔b2 ♘e7 3 ♔a2 ♔c4 4 ♔a3 ♔d5 5 ♔a4 ♔e6 6 ♔a5 ♔f7 7 ♔a6 ♘c8. The knight was relocated to facilitate this move which leaves both the knight and the a-pawn immune to capture from the white monarch. Note that 6 g8=♕+ ♘xg8 7 ♔a5 ♘e7 8 ♔a6 ♘c8 would also have seen Black back in the nick of time (you can see though why it was so important not to advance his a-pawn earlier). Of course from here he can enjoy squeezing out the white king at his leisure and then advance his a-pawn with the knight available to control a1 at the right moment.

Q5

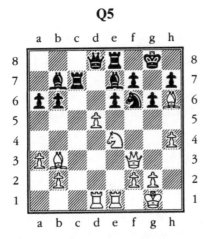

Indeed, 23 moves into the game Kamsky-Short, PCA Candidates Semi-Finals, Linares, 1994, the position above was reached (after 23 d5!)

Play continued with 23...♘xe4 24 dxe6! f5 25 ♖xd8 ♖xd8 26 ♖d1 1-0.

Scrutinizing the alternative captures on d5 we have:

a) 23...♘xd5 24 ♗xd5 ♗xd5 25 ♖xd5! exd5 (or 25...♕xd5 26 ♘f6+ ♗xf6 27 ♕xf6) 26 ♘f6+ ♗xf6 27 ♖xe8+ ♕xe8 28 ♕xf6 ♖c1+ 29 ♔h2 ♕b8+ 30 g3 with big things happening on g7!

b) 23...exd5 24 ♘xf6+ ♗xf6 25 ♕xf6 ♖xe1+ 26 ♖xe1 ♕xf6 27 ♖e8 mate.

c) 23...♗xd5 24 ♘xf6+ ♗xf6 25 ♗xd5 exd5 26 ♕xf6 as above.

As 23...e5 24 d6 ♗xe4 25 ♗xf7+ (or 25 ♖xe4) 25...♔xf7 26 ♕b3+ also looks powerful, the conclusion for 5 points must be **A**.

Q6

An important endgame to know; 2 drawing ideas are:

1 ♖g1 ♖d1 2 ♖g2+ ♔c1 (or 2...♔d3 3 ♖g3+ ♔c4 4 ♖g4+ ♖d4 5 ♖g8 when the checks can't be satisfactorily avoided) 3 ♔b3 ♖d3 4 ♖g1+ and

1 ♖h8 ♔c1+ 2 ♔b3 c2 3 ♔c3! ♔b1 3 ♖b8+ ♔c1 4 ♖h8.

However bad is 1 ♖h3? ♔c1+ 2 ♔b3 c2 3 ♖h1+ (This time there are no saving checks on the b-file after 3 ♔c3 ♔b1) 3...♖d1 4 ♖h2 ♖d3+ 5 ♔a2 (no better is 5 ♔c4 ♖g3 when the pawn will easily queen) 5...♖d8 6 ♖g2 ♖a8+ 7 ♔b3 ♔b1 8 ♖xc2 ♖b8+ 9 ♔c3 ♖c8+ winning the rook.).

The answer for 5 points is **A**.

Q7

This is a fairly straightforward one. Our quiz position was reached after 23 moves of the encounter Sadler-Condie, BCF Championship, Swansea 1995. Allegedly, backward bishop moves are the hardest type of moves to find but with 23 ♖d6 also probably adequate, the super GM had no difficulty locating 23 ♗d6 ♖xd6 24 ♕e8+ ♔h7 25 ♕xb8 1-0.

The white queen would only need to be conceded after 25...♖g6+ 26 ♕g3 (C was a red herring!) but it would reappear soon!

D earns the maximum 5 points and again nothing for anything else.

Q8

After the rather different opening sequence 1 f4 d5 2 b3 ♗g4 3 h3 ♗h5 the interesting (even if I say so myself!) game Christensen-Ward, Copenhagen 2001 saw 4 g4 e5!? 5 ♗g2 ♗g6 6 f5

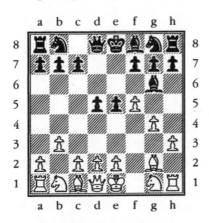

6...♗xf5! 7 gxf5 ♛h4+ 8 ♔f1 ♛f4+ 9 ♔e1 (Black regains the piece after 9 ♘f3 e4 10 d3 ♛xf5) 9...♛g3+ 10 ♔f1 ♛f4+ 11 ♔e1 ♗e7 12 ♘f3 e4 13 d3 ♛g3+ 14 ♔f1 exf3 15 exf3 ♛e5 16 d4 ♛xf5 with a clear advantage to Black.

Although at first 4...♗g6 5 f5?! e6 may appear to drop a piece to 6 h4 (intending 7 h5) in fact 6...♗e7 would seem to more than save the day. e.g. 7 ♘f3 exf5 8 h5 fxg4. I'm going to award 2 points for C and a further 2 for D which also avoids falling behind in material. However the convincing practical encounter above results in 5 points for **E**.

Q9

Very well done if you found (or knew!) the correct defence of 1 ♖b1! g5 2 ♔d3 ♖e8 3 ♖g1

The above diagram depicts the important 'frontal defence' and the idea of utilizing just enough checking distance to halt the pawn in its tracks without the use of the cut-off king. 3...♚h5 4 ♖h1+ ♚g4 (or 4...♚g6 5 ♖g1) 5 ♖g1+ ♚f4 6 ♖f1+ ♚g3 7 ♖g1+.

If you didn't, then don't panic too much as you are in good company. In the game Tal-Zaitsev, Riga 1966, White played 1 ♚d3 which loses to 1...♖e1! 2 ♚d2 ♖e8 3 ♖b1 g5 4 ♖g1 ♚h5 5 ♖h1+ ♚g6 6 ♖g1 ♖e5! (protecting the g-pawn to enable the black king to advance) 7 ♚d3 ♚f5 8 ♚d4 (or 8 ♖f1+ ♚g4 9 ♚d4 ♖a5 10 ♚e3 ♖a3+ 11 ♚e2 ♖a2+ 12 ♚e3 ♚h3 with a clear route home for the g-pawn) 8...♖e4+ 9 ♚d3 g4 10 ♖f1+ ♖f4 11 ♚e2 g3 12 ♖xf4 ♚xf4 13 ♚e1 ♚e3 with a won king and pawn ending.

Clearly one needs to be familiar with the 'Lucena' position (see below) to fully comprehend this one and, along with A, I'm generously awarding 1 point to C despite something like:

1 ♖b8 ♚h5 2 ♖h8+ ♚g4 3 ♖g8 g5 4 ♚d3 ♖e7 5 ♚d2 ♚f4 6 ♖f8+ ♚g3 7 ♖g8 g4 8 ♖g6 ♚f3 9 ♖f6+ ♚g2 10 ♖g6 g3 11 ♖g8 ♚f2 12 ♖f8+ ♚g1 13 ♖g8 g2 14 ♖h8 ♖e5!

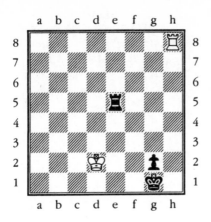

15 ♖h7 ♔f2 16 ♖f7+ ♔g3 17 ♖g7+ ♔f3 0-1

Naturally 5 points go to the choice of **B**.

Q10

Things are looking pretty grim for White but he can salvage a draw with the clever 1 ♖f5 ♕xe6 2 ♖xe5! ♕xe5 3 a3.

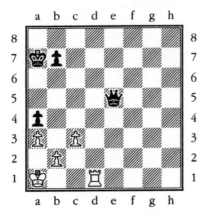

His next move will be 4 ♖d4 when, able to oscillate between b4 and d4, White will have erected a barrier to prevent the black king advancing down the board. It was important to stop Black getting in ...a3, mixing things up, and the whole concept produces a satisfactory blockade.

5 points for **C**.

Q11

With 5 points for **B** one can't really argue with 1 ♖xf8+! ♚xf8 (mate follows quickly after 1...♕xf8 i.e. 2 ♗h7+ ♚h8 3 ♗g6+ ♚g8 4 ♕h7) 2 ♕h8+ ♚f7 3 ♗g6+!! ♚e6 (or of course 3...♚xg6 4 ♕h5 mate) 4 ♕g8+ ♚d7 5 ♗f5+.

This neat combination was seen in the game Geller-Novotelnov, Moscow 1951.

Q12

It is pure folly for Black to consider giving up a piece for two pawns right now, thus ruling out A and B. Although 1...c5 2 ♘xc5 ♗xc5 3 ♕xc5 ♕d1+ comes to nothing, in arguably Grandmaster Keith Arkell's finest moment, against GM Gdanski in the European team championships 2000, he came up with the inspirational 1...g5!!. Bemusing at first, his motives soon become clear. White must do something to avoid having his kingside pawn structure irrevocably weakened but check out: 2 hxg5 (2 h5 would receive the same treatment) 2...c5 3 ♘xc5 (Objectively, I suppose 3 f4 now is more of a winning attempt but then the queenside pawns are liquidated and the black queen gets to infiltrate White's airy kingside) 3...♗xc5 4 ♕xc5 ♕d1+ 5 ♚g2

Different from the previous position, above Black now has 5...♘f4+! which after 6 gxf4 (upon 6 ♚h2 there is always 6...♕h5+) 6...♕g4+ 7 ♚f1 ♕d1+ with a perpetual check.

5 points for **D**.

Q13

From our quiz position, play in Scalcione-Cebalo, Reggio Emilia 2001, continued with 1...♘xe4! 2 fxe4 ♗xd4 3 ♘xd4 ♛xc3!!

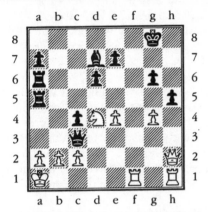

Although neither suggestions A nor B would have worked, clearly both ideas came into play in this visual combination. Now, in view of the mate down the a-file with the two rooks, White threw in the towel. 5 points for **C**.

Q14

In the recent game Hebden-Kiriakov, Hastings Premier 2002, Black found himself in severe time trouble and thus with little time to ponder the last two moves before the 40 move time control. Doing the commentary on the event I was very critical of Mr Kiriakov's judgement call at the time although, as he correctly pointed out later, when your flag is hanging, you are hardly at your most logical.

From our quiz position (repeated above) play continued:

39...♖b6 40 ♖c8+ ♔h7 41 ♖c7 ♖f6 42 b4 g5 43 hxg6+ ♔xg6 44 b5 axb5 45 axb5 h5 46 ♖e7 h4 47 c4 h3 48 ♔a3 ♔g5 49 ♖e1 h2 50 c5 ♖h6 51 ♖h1 ♔f6 52 b6 ♔e7 53 b7 ♖h8 54 ♖xh2 ♖b8 55 c6 ♔d6 56 ♖h6+ ♔c7 57 ♖f6 ♖g8 58 ♔b4 ♔b6 59 ♔c4 ♖d8 60 ♔c3 ♖e8 61 ♔d4 ♖d8+ 62 ♔c4 ♖e8 63 ♔d5 ♖d8+ 64 ♖d6 ♖f8 65 ♖d7 f5 66 c7 ♔xb7 67 ♖d8 1-0

Although Black's h-pawn was quick, it was easily blockaded and the best type of passed pawns to have in rook endings are connected ones. A defending rook is much more likely to be able to concede itself for two isolated pawns than for a couple that can advance in tandem. Although the relative positions up/down the board the opposing passed pawns are in is obviously a critical factor, it is clear that White's queenside pawns were monsters.

Although 39...f5 would have got a pawn under way, White's h-pawn (too time-consuming to remove) would have prevented a partnership with the g-pawn. Clearly 39...♖b6 was employed to prevent, say 39...g5 40 ♖c6 or 40 hxg6 fxg6 41 ♖c6. However I believe that that was the correct route to go down. Indeed after, say 39...g5 40 ♖c6 ♔g7 41 ♖xa6 f5 42 ♖g6+ ♔h7 43 b4 f4 44 a5 ♖f8, Black's pawns are faster than Black whereas 39...g5 40 hxg6 fxg6 41 ♖c6 ♔g7 42 ♖xa6 h5 43 b4 h4 would also see Black's rook the best temporary defender and the h-pawn the most menacing of all of the passed pawns.

Essentially the point I'm making is that three connected passed pawns aren't necessarily much better than two connected passed pawns when there is no defending king available as a rook has little chance of being able to give itself up for the two anyhow.

1...g6 would be a tempo slower as ...gxh5 isn't desirable anyway. I'm going to give 1 point for D as that was Grandmaster Kiriakov's choice under pressure although he later acknowledged that **B** (for 5 points) was a far superior solution.

Q15

I'll generously award a point for C but full marks go to **A** with the game Gross-Borgo, Hotel Agro, Budapest 1999, finishing nicely with: 1 ♗g7+! ♗xg7 2 ♖xh7+!.

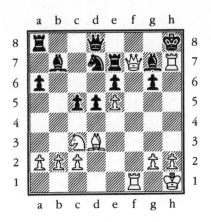

Black resigned in view of 2...♔xh7 3 ♕xg6+ ♔g8 4 ♕h7 mate.

Q16

I hope I didn't mislead you too much in the phrasing of the question particularly as the wording of C, D and E was completely irrelevant! For 5 points the answer is **A** as the analysis below proves:

a) 1 ♔c2 b1=♕+! 2 ♔xb1 ♔d3 3 ♔a1 ♔c2 with 4...♗b2 mate next go.

b) 1 d3+ ♔e3 2 ♔c2 (or 2 d4 ♔d3 3 d5 ♔c3 4 d6 ♗xd6) 2...♔d4 3 ♔b1 ♔c3 4 d4 ♔d3 5 d5 ♔c3 6 d6 ♗xd6 with an easy win e.g. 7 a4 ♗c7 8 a5 ♗xa5 9 ♔a2 ♔c2.

c) 1 d4 ♔d3 2 d5 ♔c3 3 d6 ♗xd6 which transposes to the above.

Q17

Well, congratulations to all those who chose E but did you really think that you would get any points? If you did I'm afraid you are very mistaken as for a reason that I can't really explain why I am awarding a bonus point for C. I suppose it's because Black does have plenty of good moves in our quiz position but full marks go to B based in main on the game continuation of Gurevich-Kaufman, Seattle 2002:

1...♕xc1! 2 ♖xc1 ♖d1+ 3 ♔h2 ♖xc1 4 ♕f4

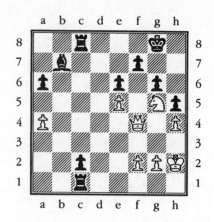

White threatens both mate via 5 ♕xf7+ as well as the rook on c1 but Black had things all under control with 4...♖h1+! 5 ♔g3 (or 5 ♔xh1 c1=♕ which is of course check!) 5...♖f8. As White's attacking aspirations had been halted and an enemy promotion was imminent, he promptly resigned.

Q18

My analysis from the quiz knight endgame position runs:

a) 1 h5 gxh5 2 ♘xh7 (2 ♘xh5 ♔g6 3 ♘f6 ♔xf4 4 ♘xh7 ♔xe5 is certainly no better for White) when at the very least 2...♔xf4 3 ♘xf8 ♔xg5 4 ♘xe6+ ♔f5 5 ♘g7+ sees Black draw.

b) 1 f5 exf5 (And not 1...♔f4?? which is disastrous in view of 2 ♘xh7 ♘xh7 3 fxg6) 2 ♘xh7 ♘e6 when Black has the upper hand.

c) 1 ♔c3 ♔xf4 2 ♔d4 ♔f5 3 ♘e8 ♔g4 when, if anyone, Black has the edge.

d) 1 ♘xh7! ♘xh7 2 h5 ♘f8 (2...♔xf4 3 hxg6 ♘f8 4 g7 is even more straightforward) 3 f5!

100

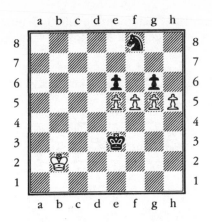

3...exf5 (or 3...gxf5 4 g6 when the g-pawn can't be stopped.) 4 h6 f4 5 h7 (Alternatively 5 e6 ♘xe6 6 h7 which should also be winning) 5...♘xh7 6 e6 and White queens first with check, e.g. 6...f3 7 e7 f2 8 e8=♕+ ♚d2 9 ♕b5 ♚e1 10 ♕e5+ ♚d2 11 ♕f4+ ♚e2 12 ♕e4+ ♚d2 13 ♕f3 ♚e1 14 ♕e3+ ♚f1 15 ♚c2 etc.

My conclusion then; 1 point for A because that's the sort of guy I am but 5 points for **D**.

Q19

After consulting my rather large database of top level games I can inform you that 5...♗e7 and 5...h6 are the most popular moves in our quiz position. As 5...♗b4 would be a direct transposition to a 'Nimzo-Indian' defence then that is obviously acceptable too.

Grandmasters are generally not that eager to concede bishops (particularly fianchettoed ones) for knights without good reason and hence the unprovoked 5...♗xf3?! can't be good.

Clearly 5...c5?! leads to a poor 'Benoni' defence after 6 d5 as Black's light-squared bishop would be locked out of serious action on b7. Aside from a possible ...♘xd5 trick (i.e. contesting the e7-h4 diagonal), Black's other bishop would be passively placed on e7 too (it would prefer a kingside fianchetto).

The key to this question revolves around the move 5...d5. Although on the face of it this may look like a reasonable move, transposing into some sort of Queen's Gambit Declined, in the game

Ward-H.Hunt, British Championship 2000, I observed a way to exploit a black move order that had not yet included unpinning the f6-knight:

1 d4 ♘f6 2 c4 e6 3 ♘f3 b6 4 ♘c3 ♗b7 5 ♗g5 d5?! 6 cxd5 exd5 7 ♕a4+!

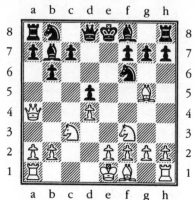

The text is an awkward move to deal with. Above 7...c6 would be met by 8 ♗xf6 as 8...♕xf6 allows 9 ♘xd5. If 7...♘bd7 then 8 ♘e5 seeks to exploit the c6-square as well as maintaining pressure on both d7 and f6. As 7...♗c6 would have left the bishop poorly placed after either 8 ♕b3 or 8 ♕c2, it is no surprise that Harriet selected 7...♕d7. However after 8 ♗xf6 ♕xa4 9 ♘xa4 gxf6 10 e3 ♗d6 11 ♖c1 a6 12 ♘h4!? White had effectively been gifted with a significant structural advantage because of Black's 5th move inaccuracy.

Taking all of the above on board, I'm giving a point for C and D but 5 for **E**.

Q20

Provided the white king moves to the g-file then it will be in range of the enemy pawn (ruling out A). Checking out the options:

a) 1 ♔g3 enables Black to simply obtain the opposition and he might win say after 1...♔g5 2 ♔f3 ♔f5 3 ♔e3 ♔e5 4 ♔d3 ♔d5 5 ♔c3 ♔c5 6 ♔b3 ♔b5 7 ♔a3 ♔c4 8 ♔b2 ♔b4 9 ♔a2 ♔c3 10 ♔b1 ♔b3 11 ♔c1 b5 12 ♔b1 b4 13 ♔a1 ♔c2 14 ♔a2 b3+ 15 ♔a1 b2+.

b) Over-finessing somewhat is 1 ♔g1 as after, say 1...♚g5 2 ♔f1 ♚f4 3 ♔f2 ♚e4 4 ♔e2 ♚d4 5 ♔d2 ♚c4 6 ♔c2 ♚b4 7 ♔b2, Black wins by using his b-pawn to help regain the opposition i.e. 7...b5. There wasn't much substance in White's argument anyway though, as 2...♚f5 would also have won. Also don't forget that if the attacking king can get in front of the passed pawn (excluding a rook's pawn) on the 6ᵗʰ rank then he wins whoever is to move.

c) 1 ♔g2! ♚g6 (or 1...♚g5 2 ♔g3) 2 ♔f2 ♚f6 (or 2...♚f5 3 ♔f3; note the emerging pattern) 3 ♔e2 ♚e6 4 ♔d2 ♚d6 5 ♔c2 ♚c6 6 ♔b2

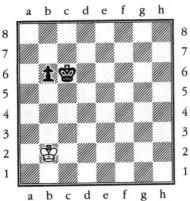

Here White is well positioned to obtain the opposition. Upon 6...♚b5 there is 7 ♔b3, 6...♚c5 should see 7 ♔c3 and 6...♚d5 should receive the diagonal treatment of 7 ♔b3 too. This line is a draw and hence 5 points for **C**.

Test Two: Answers

Q1

Suggestions A and B just don't remotely work whilst 21...♕d5 is adequately met by 22 ♗f2 e.g. 22...♖8e3 (or 22...♗f5 23 ♖fd1) 23 ♕xe3 ♖xe3 24 ♗xe3 ♕xc6 25 ♖ac1 with a comfortable edge to White.

Critical is 21...♕g5 when after 22 ♖f2 ♗h3 White has the visual defence of 23 ♗f8!

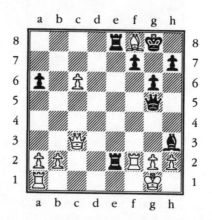

Here, obviously, mate is threatened on g7 and it is clear that 23...♔xf8 loses to 24 ♕h8+ whilst 23...♖xf8 allows 24 ♖xe2 immediately. With the bishop no longer attacked on c5, Black's light-squared bishop is hanging and for example 23...♕e5 (also note 23...f6 24 ♕c4+!) 24 ♖xe2! (even better than 24 ♕xe5) 24...♕xc3 25 bxc3 ♖xe2 26 gxh3 ♔xf8 27 c7 ♖e8 28 ♖b1 is a neat win.

5 points for **E**.

Q2

In the game Kalezic-Popadic, Montenegro Championship, Tivat 2000, play continued with:

21 ♘xf7! ♗xf7 22 ♖xf7!

This comprises a devastating attack and indeed 22...♖xf7 23 ♖xf7 ♔xf7 24 ♕xh7+ ♔f8 (or 24 ..♔f6 25 ♕xg6 mate) 25 ♗xg6 left Black with no option to resign in view of the next up mate on either f7 or h8.

There are 5 points for **C** but I'm going to award 3 points for 21 ♖xf7 (i.e. **D**) as although Black has more options, the likes of 21...♗xf7 (21...♖xf7 22 ♘xf7 ♗f8 23 ♕xf8+ leads to a winning ending) 22 ♘xf7 ♕e8 23 ♗xg6 still looks pretty effective!

Q3

In this wonderful 1923 study by Troitzky a draw can be proved by:

1 ♘f2+ ♔g3 (Moving the king anywhere else would see the c-pawn queening with check) 2 c7 a2 (And certainly not 2...h1=♕+?? 3 ♘xh1+ i.e. it is taken with check!) 3 ♘e4+! ♔f3 (The key is that this is forced in view of 3...♔h4 4 cxd8=♕+ and 3...♔h3 4 c8=♕+) 4 ♘d2+ ♔e3 (instead 4...♔g3 5 ♘e4+ merely repeats the position) 5 ♘c4+ ♔e4 6 ♘d2+ ♔e5 7 ♘c4+

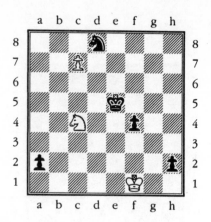

Here, remarkably, Black can't avoid the white knight checks without walking into either cxd8=♕ or c8=♕, both check!

Throwing in the towel too soon wouldn't have earned you the draw or the 5 points that the selection of **B** does.

Q4

In Tebb-Ward, British Championship 1998, I reached our quiz position in definitely one of my best ever games. In this situation one knows what one wants to do, it's just a matter of side-stepping the files and diagonals of the defending pieces. When I confidently bashed out (?!) my 28th move I had 5 minutes left on the clock to reach the 40 move time control (or force some sort of result)...

There is some logic to all of the suggestions but although 28...♕b1+ 29 ♖d1 ♕b4+ 30 ♖d2 ♕b1+ should be a draw, instead I found:

28...♕e6+! 29 ♖e4 (Forced in view of 29...♕e2+) 29...♕a2!

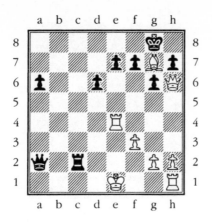

Phase 2! As the white rook is no longer on the d-file, it is unavailable to stop 30...♛b1+.

Hence White tried 30 ♔f1 (Now Black has seventh heaven, there is no time to return, i.e. 30 ♖d4 ♖e2+ 31 ♔f1 ♖f2+ 32 ♔g1 ♖xg2+ 33 ♔f1 ♛f2 mate) but 30...♖f2+ 31 ♔e1 ♖xg2! was most effective. Again a 'lawnmower' style checkmate is threatened via a queen to the 8th rank and after 32 ♛c1 ♛f2+ 33 ♔d1 ♛xf3+ White resigned as the e4-rook would drop, with mate following.

1 point for C but 5 for **D**.

Q5

A is obviously a queen blunder but I will award a point each for B, C and D. They are all sensible queen moves but offering White by far the most is:

13 ♛h5+! g6 14 ♘xe4! gxh5 (Somewhat falling in with White's plans but he would hardly complain about 14 ..fxe4 15 ♛e5 ♖f8 16 ♛xe4 either!) 15 ♘f6+ ♔f8 16 ♗h6 mate!

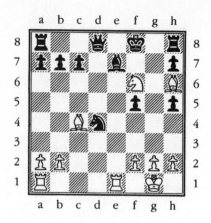

Not a bad position to end a game with (so long as you're not Black!). 5 points for **E**.

Q6

Our quiz position occurred in the game Genov-S.Ivanov, Berlin Sommer tournament 1993.

First up, 1...♘d4??, presumably hoping for 2 ♘xd4?? ♛xg2 mate, simply drops a piece to 2 ♛xd4.

Black's kingside is already devoid of defenders and although 1...g5? 2 ♘xg5 ♛xe5 might be playable, the simple 2 ♛f6! is just very strong for White.

I hope you observed the d1-rook uncovering concept of ♗h7+. That therefore rules out D but on the other hand the positional sacrifice involved in 1...♖fd8 is quite interesting:

2 ♗h7+ ♚xh7 3 ♖xd5 ♖xd5 (it's nice to have a piece on d5) 4 h4.

Here there is no longer a serious kingside attack available to White and, as well as not actually being material down, Black is in control of the centre of the board and has a handy extra queenside pawn.

Both 4...♔g8 and 4...♖d7 leave Black looking with optimism towards the endgame.

Although I'm therefore giving 5 points for **C**, I do feel that the trick-avoiding 1...♕a5 should be rewarded too (hence 3 points for **E**). Although 2 ♕e4 g6 3 ♕f4 looks dangerous e.g. 3...♔h7 4 ♗xg6+! fxg6 (or 4...♔xg6 5 ♕f6+ ♔h7 6 ♘g5+!! hxg5 7 ♖d3 with mate inevitable) 5 ♖d7+ ♔g8 6 ♕xh6, things aren't that clear after 3...♘e7.

Q7

Although in England the late Tony Miles was renowned for his long grinds, he always kept an eye out for beautiful tactics. In the Dublin zonal tournament of 1993 against Grandmaster Aaron Summerscale he found:

1 ♗b4! ♕xb4 (Black can't even sneak away with just the loss of the exchange e.g. 1...♕d8 2 ♗xf8 ♔xf8 [note 2...♕xd4+ 3 ♔h1 ♔xf8 4 ♖ad1 is crushing] 3 ♕c5+ ♔g8 4 ♘xf6+ ♕xf6 5 ♖e8+ ♔h7 6 ♗c2+ g6 7 ♕f8) 2 ♘xf6+ gxf6 3 ♕g6+.

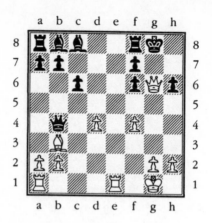

This is the position after a key move in the combination that takes advantage of the pinned f-pawn. After 3...♔h8 4 ♕xh6+ ♔g8 5 ♕g6+ ♔h8 6 ♕xf6+ (Tony would have loved these checks!) 6...♔g8 the next critical insertion was 7 ♖e3.

With 8 ♖g3+ up next, Black resigned leaving me to award the maximum 5 points to **B**.

Of the alternatives given, I will donate 2 points to E as that would have left White with an edge too and is the sort of continuation that Tony would have employed were it not for this excellent forcing sequence.

Q8

I must confess that this was a tough one!

1 ♔e2 ♔b3 2 ♔d3 ♔a4 isn't winning but the fantastic variation below is:

1 ♗g1 ♗g3 (Note that Black can't trade bishops as after 1...♗xg1 2 ♔xg1 ♔b3 3 g4 fxg3 4 f4 ♔c4 5 f5 one of White's f- or e-pawns will promote.) 2 ♗h2!! (A truly delightful concept. Now, as before, 2...♔b3 3 ♗xg3 fxg3 f4 will see a white pawn queen whilst 2...♗h4 simply drops the f4-pawn.) 2...♗xh2 3 g4! (The point. Due to the presence of a white pawn on e5, now the black bishop is unable to swing back to halt the g-pawn in time.) 3...fxg3 4 ♔g2!

110

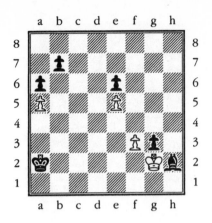

(Preventing Black from inserting the bishop freeing ...g2+.) 4...♔b3 5 f4 ♔c4 6 f5 ♔d5 7 f6 and victory is close. As in the previous sidelines the black king was too slow in returning to fulfill an essential task.

5 points for **A**.

Q9

It's debatable which of 1 ♖gf4 c1=♕ 2 ♖xc1 ♖xc1+ 3 ♖f1 ♖xf1+ 4 ♔xf1 ♘g4 5 ♔e2 ♘xh2 6 ♔d3 ♔f8 or

1 ♗xf7+ ♔h8! 2 ♖gf4 c1=♕ 3 ♖xc1 ♖xc1+ 4 ♖f1 (the fork 4 ♔f2 ♘d3+ is not to be forgotten) 4...♖xf1+ 5 ♔xf1 ♘xf7 is the best practical try but clearly both are losing.

As 1 ♖xf7 ♘xf7 is also hopeless and I can't see anything else, there is really little substance to this question (sorry did I trick you?) and you get 5 points if you correctly selected **A**.

Q10

In the game Kramnik-Short, Dortmund 1995, the current world champion (well one of them!) found the bonecrushing 1 ♗xe6!! fxe6 2 ♕xg6.

111

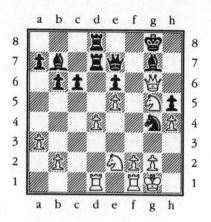

Here Black is completely paralyzed and can only await the lethal introduction of the e2-knight. That didn't take long and indeed play terminated after 2...♘xe5 3 ♕h7+ ♚f8 4 ♘f4 1-0

It would have paid to notice that moving the g5-knight in our quiz position might allow the embarrassing 1...♕xh4 and I am going to award 2 points for A (1 ♘f4) as that does look quite promising. Of course **D** gets the full 5 points.

Q11

Okay the truth and nothing but the truth is that after 1...♗xg5 Black is threatening 1...♗f6 mate. Now although 2 ♕f1 a1=♕ is winning for Black, there is another defence in the form of 2 g8=♘!. Suddenly it's looking grim for Black but he has a trick in 2...♗e3 (read on for how White should respond to 2...♗d2)

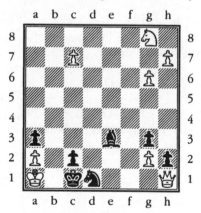

Here if White prevents the threat of 3...♗d4 mate with 3 h8=♕ then 3...♗d4+ 4 ♕xd4 is stalemate. However White has the clever 3 h8=♗!

Then Black's only chance lies with 3...♗d2 as 4 c8=♕ ♗c3+ would still lead to stalemate. Alas (and I'm sure you're observing the pattern by now!) White has 4 c8=♖ which prepares to capture on c3 with the rook. In ...♔d2 there is an unwanted move and so White will have successfully utilized 3 successive under-promotions. Not perhaps your every day occurrence but nevertheless I'm still sorry if you chose E! That scenario is regrettable but I guess it's tough luck and by the way **D** gets the 5 points.

I suppose one could argue that A would have been applicable if Black hadn't tested White and so I'll reluctantly award 2 points for that too.

Q12

They all seem to be much of a muchness but, whilst eager to get at White's 2 remaining pawns, each of A, B, D and E are all very plausible, winning by force is:

1...b3! 2 ♖xb3 (forced or else a pawn would promote via 2...♘e2 or 2...♘d3) 2...♘e2! 3 ♔xc2 ♘d4+ 4 ♔c3 ♘xb3 5 ♔xb3 ♔f6 6 ♔c3 (or 6 ♔c4) 6...♔e5 7 ♔d3 ♔f4. This neat bit of tactical play earns Black a won king and pawn ending and selectors of **C** a deserved 5 points.

Q13

It has to be said that the suggestions of C, D and E are all very reasonable but alas I won't award any points there. Look on the bright side though. I should really be deducting points for 1 ♗xg7? as it just doesn't work. True there is something to be said for 1...♗xe4? 2 ♕f6 but 1...♔xg7 isn't that risky as advancing the f-pawn will be a timely defence e.g. 2 ♕g4+ ♔h8 3 ♗xh7 f5! and the attack will be rebuffed.

On the other hand in Miles-Browne, Lucerne Olympiad 1982, with reference to question 7 in this same test, Tony was up to his old tricks again:

1 ♗xh7+!! ♔xh7 2 ♕h5+ ♔g8 3 ♗xg7! (phase 2 and the correct position in which to make this sac)

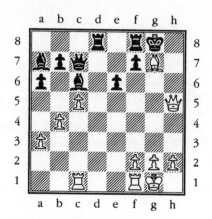

A theme that should hopefully stick in your mind now, the critical rook swing came after 3...♔xg7 (Note after 3...f6 4 ♕h8+ ♔f7 5 ♗xf8 Black can't recapture the bishop because of 6 ♕h7+) 4 ♕g5+ ♔h8 5 ♕f6+ ♔g8 6 ♖c4.

Yes it's the same old story and **B** gets the 5 points.

Q14

Having, I believe, performed quite well in the encounter Ward-Brameld, Jersey 1999, and played 31 ♖1c4, I suddenly started having palpitations as I noticed the concept of 31...♖bb1 (anything else e.g. 31...♖d8 is pretty hopeless) 31 ♖h4+ ♕h5. Just as I was trying to work out whether I had blundered horribly, my opponent resigned. I can tell you what a relief that was at a time although a close inspection reveals that in fact after 32 ♖xh5+ gxh5 33 g4 (the only way to stop the mate on h1) 33...h4 34 g3

114

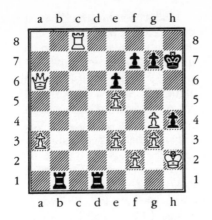

Black has nothing. e.g. 34...h3 35 ♔xh3 ♖h1+ 36 ♔g2 ♖bg1+ 37 ♔f3.

There was no perpetual check or drawish rook ending. Certainly no mating net and so, ignoring the reasonable but non-rewardable option E, there are 5 points for **A**.

Q15

The following variations should prove rather instructive and will certainly throw some light on this question:

a) 1...♔d8 2 ♔f3! ♔e7

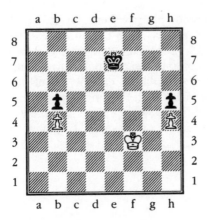

3 ♔e3! (White's idea is simple: if Black attempts to keep his distance he will lose one of his pawns, with his own king being well behind in the race to capture the enemy pawn on the opposite side of the board, and White will make a new queen. It is very important to note that Black can get a suitable opposition after 3 ♔f4 ♚f6 and the text is far more subtle.) 3...♚e6 4 ♔e4. As White has your basic opposition a win is straightforward e.g. 4...♚d6 5 ♔d4! (Both sides would get a queen after 5 ♔f5 ♚d5 6 ♔g5 ♚c4 7 ♔xh5 ♚xb4 but White is careful to ensure that he gets a significant lead in the race.) 5...♚c6 (or 5...♚e6 6 ♔c5) 6 ♔e5 (It's the b-pawn White is after and the black king will be nudged away from protecting it.) 6...♚c7 7 ♔d5 ♚b6 8 ♔d6 ♚b7 9 ♔c5 ♚a6 10 ♔c6 ♚a7 11 ♔xb5 ♚b7 12 ♔c5 ♚c7 13 ♔d5 ♚b6 14 ♔e5 ♚b5 15 ♔f5 ♚xb4 16 ♔g5 ♚c5 17 ♔xh5 ♚d6 18 ♔g6 ♚e7 19 ♔g7 and the h-pawn promotes.

b) 1...♚e7 2 ♔e3 ♚f6 (other moves transpose to variation a) 3 ♔f4! ♚g6 (or 3...♚e6 4 ♔g5) 4 ♔e5 ♚h6 5 ♔f6 ♚h7 6 ♔g5 ♚g7 7 ♔xh5 ♚h7 8 ♔g5 ♚g7 9 ♔f5. White nabs the b-pawn and wins.

c) 1...♚f7 2 ♔f3! ♚e7 3 ♔e3! when if Black now advances to the 3rd rank White will take the opposition, while remaining on the 2nd rank will receive the diagonally forward treatment with White winning a pawn well in advance of his opponent.

Surprising stuff (or was it?). 5 points for **E**.

Q16

Although a common plan for Black when White sets up a bind (i.e. with pawns on e4 and c4) as in our quiz question is to break free of the shackles with ...b5 or ...d5, neither of those continuations would work here. I am going to award 2 points for D and 3 points for E but for the maximum score check out the recent impressive encounter Eames-Emms, 4NCL 2002. A serious plan that White has in the position is h4 and then g5. To prevent that and add some extra spice to the game, Grandmaster (and sort of co-author of the *Chess Choice Challenge* 1st volume) John Emms unleashed: 16...♘h7! 17 ♕f2 g5!

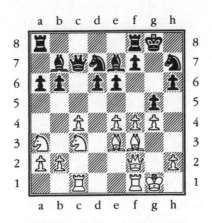

(Another point behind Black's last move and an important thematic concept. Black fights to gain control of the e5-square; an excellent post for a black knight.) 18 ♖fd1 gxf4 19 ♗xf4 ♘e5!? 20 ♗xh6 ♘g5 21 ♗xg5 (Noting 21 ♗g2? ♘xg4 it becomes clear that the text move is forced. White has his extra pawn but Black's compensation includes general control of the dark squares.) 21 ...♗xg5 22 ♖c2 f5!? 23 gxf5 exf5 24 ♗h5?! (In truth 24 ♘d5 would offer a better defence although the opening of the f-file is still a daunting prospect for White to have to face.) 24...♕g7 25 ♕g2 fxe4 26 ♖xd6 ♘f3+! 27 ♔h1 (If 27 ♗xf3 then 27...exf3 28 ♕g3 ♗e3+ 29 ♔f1 ♗c8!, with ...♗h3+ in mind, is very strong.) 27...♘e1 28 ♕h3 (Or 28 ♕g1 e3+ 29 ♘d5 ♘xc2 30 ♖g6 ♕xg6 31 ♗xg6 e2 32 ♘xc2 ♖f1 which is game over!) 28...♗c8! 29 ♖e6 ♗xe6 30 ♕xe6+ ♔h8 31 ♕h3 ♕h6 32 ♖e2 ♖f3 0-1.

5 points for **C**.

Q17

I'm going to award 5 points for **B** which is justified by the continuation of Timman-Gelfand, Wijk aan Zee 2002:

1 ♖c6! ♗b7 2 cxd5! ♗xc6 3 dxc6 ♔d6

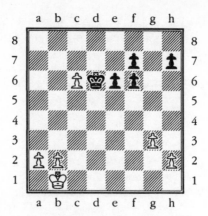

4 g4. White has a won king and pawn endgame with the last move of the game (i.e Black resigned here) being very tidy as it ensures that, with his pawn majority, Black can only guarantee a supported passed pawn on the 4th rank. That is not far enough and play may have continued:

4...♚xc6 5 ♔c2 ♚d5 6 ♔d3 ♚c5 7 ♔c3 ♚b5 8 b4 ♚a4 9 ♔c4 e5 10 b5 ♚a5 11 a4 ♚b6 12 ♔b4 ♚b7 13 a5 ♚c7 14 ♔c5 ♚b7 15 b6 ♚b8 16 a6 ♚c8 17 ♔c6 e4 18 b7+ ♚b8 19 ♔b6 e3 20 a7 mate!

Probably winning for Black is 1 ♖xd5 and I will award 2 points for C although if winning, it is far from trivial.

Q18

You should really have got this one as it's quite straightforward:

a) 1 ♔f1 ♚d2 2 ♔g1 ♚e2 3 ♔h1 f3

4 gxf3 (Or 4 ♔g1 f2+ 5 ♔h1 f1=♕ mate) 4...♔f2 and, as the presence of the white f-pawn ensures that it's not stalemate, the g-pawn will promote real soon!

b) 1 ♔h1 ♔d3 2 ♔g1 ♔e2 3 ♔h1 f3 with the same story as above.

5 points for **D**.

Q19

I think that both A and B deserve a point each but regarding **C** (5 points), it certainly does! The game Kiriakov-Baburin, Isle Of Man 2001, witnessed 7 ♘xb5!!, with the intention being 7...♗xb5 8 ♗xc4!. Extremely beautiful, the idea being that after 8...♗xc4 although currently two pieces up, there comes 9 ♕c6+

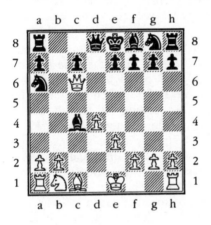

9...♕d7 10 ♕xa8+ ♕d8 11 ♕c6+ ♕d7 12 ♕xc4 would see the dust settle with Black the exchange down!

As it happens, Black tried 7...♘f6 8 ♗xc4 e6? (8...c6 would have put up greater resistance although it's still pretty grim) 9 ♕b7! c6 10 ♕xa6 cxb5 11 ♗xb5 but unsurprisingly went on to lose anyhow.

119

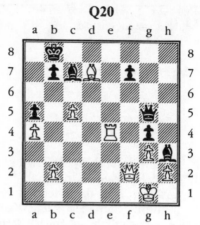

In the game Marusenko-Ward, Isle of Man 2000, the above position was reached a move prior to our quiz one. Here is my story:

On the move I am an exchange and a pawn up with Black threatening absolutely nothing. All that is required is that I make two sensible moves in order to reach the time control when Black will probably resign. 39 ♕e3 or 39 ♗b5 spring to mind with 39 ♖e8+ also eating up a move. But no, when you feel as though the outcome of the game isn't so critical (I wasn't doing so well in the tournament), the temptation is there (or at least it obviously was with me!) to finish with slightly more style. Winning though it is, a ridiculous continuation in the circumstances was 39 c6 (intending a mate with the queen, rook and bishop in the event of 39...bxc6 40 ♖e8+) 39...♗b6 (A trick which to my credit I had seen. Black's point is that 40 ♕xb6 drops the queen to 40...♕c1+ 41 ♔f2 ♕f1+ 42 ♔e3 ♕g1+, but I had it all under control.) 40 ♖e8+?? (Not with this move I didn't though. What a complete and utter idiot! I had been aware that 40 c7+ ♔xc7 41 ♖c4+ ♔xd7 42 ♕xb6 would win, as the key point was to keep c1 under lock and key, which incidentally a new queen on c8 would do. Suddenly though, with my flag hanging, I had hallucinated and found myself banging out the text.) 40...♔a7 0-1

But only after several minutes of sitting in disbelief at what had just happened. It didn't take me long to realize that 41 ♖a8+ ♔xa8 42 ♕xb6 would lose the queen through the same c1-f1-g1 checking sequence (amazing that that should be the case even though my rook is no longer on the board - NOT!).

Yes I know, it brings tears to the eyes! My conclusion; 5 points for **A**.

Test Three: Answers

Q1

The first two (very similar) lines that I'd like to demonstrate win for White are:

a) 1...♚g2 2 ♚f6 ♚f3 (obvious is 2...h1=♛ 3 ♖xh1 ♚xh1 4 ♚xg6 ♚g2 5 ♚xf5) 3 ♚g5 ♚g3 4 ♖h1 ♚g2 5 ♖xh2+ ♚xh2 6 ♚xg6 ♚g3 7 ♚xf5 and

b) 1...♚g4 2 ♖f1! ♚g3 3 ♚f6 ♚g2 4 ♖a1 h1=♛ (or 4...♚g3 5 ♚g5 ♚f3 6 ♖h1 ♚g2 7 ♖xh2+ ♚xh2 8 ♚xg6 ♚g3 9 ♚xf5) 5 ♖xh1 ♚xh1 6 ♚xg6.

In A.Ledger-Emms, National Club, England 2000, then things may have looked bad for Black until another alternative appeared:
1...♚f3!

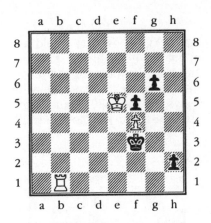

It is important that Black keeps tabs on White's f-pawn in order to prevent ♚f6 (note that wouldn't be true of 1...♚h3). There is now no way for White to win as was demonstrated by Emms in the game:

2 ♖c1 ♚g3 3 ♖f1 ♚g2 4 ♖b1 ♚f3 5 ♚f6 ♚xf4 6 ♚xg6 ♚g3 7 ♚xf5 ♚g2 8 ♖b2+ ♚g3 9 ♖xh2 ♚xh2 ½-½.

It's 5 points for **D**.

A close inspection reveals that 1 ♗xg6 fxg6 2 ♖xg6+ hxg6 3 ♕xg6+ ♔h8 4 ♕h6+ ♔g8 is only good enough for a draw as 5 ♖g1+? ♕xg1+ 6 ♘xg1 leaves Black up by too much material.

Meanwhile the logical but slower 1 h4 allows Black some time to defend e.g. 1...♖d8 2 h5 ♗f5.

After 1 ♘g5 ♗xg5 2 ♖xg5, Black can defend with 2...♕d4 but in Khalifman-Bareev, Wijk aan Zee 2002, Black actually ... resigned upon facing 1 ♖g5! The simple idea is that if Black moves his queen then the same rook nudges to h5 with an unstoppable mate. If 2...♗xg5 3 ♘xg5 then Black is forced to part with his queen rather than allow say 3...♖e8 4 ♕xh7+ ♔f8 5 ♕xf7 mate.

There is 2...f5 but then White can finish nicely with 3 ♖xg6+!! hxg6 4 ♕xg6+ ♔h8 5 ♕h6+ ♔g8 6 ♗c4+! ♕xc4 7 ♖g1+ and, in case you were wondering, it's mate in 7!

5 points for **C**.

Even though I asked YOU how you would assess the position I will award a point for E although let's face it, everyone hates it when they are trying to get at the truth and 'unclear' is all they are provided with. I'm also going to give a point for C although the game Tomczak-Bastys, World U20 Team Championship, Rio de Janeiro Brazil 2001, illustrated just how powerful the bishop-pair can be:

1...♖xc5! 2 dxc5 ♗d4!

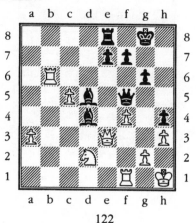

Black's plan is to lure the white queen away from the defence of the h3-pawn. Between the bishops and the queen there is no safe square along the 3ʳᵈ rank and White resigned in view of 3 ♕xd4 ♕xh3+ 4 ♔g1 ♕xg2 mate.

5 points for **D**.

Q4

Definitely nothing for 33...♔f8?? which offers White a tasty choice of 34 ♕d6+ and 34 ♕a8+. I will however reward C and D with 1 point each. Certainly D contains a good argument but I'm sure most would playing like this with the queens still on and the king exposed in the centre.

Now I'm kind of hoping that the encounter Dishman-Ward, 4NCL Birmingham 2001, is going to prove quite instructive.

After 33...♕c4! 34 ♕xc4 ♖xc4 my claim is that despite being a pawn down, Black is better. White's extra g-pawn isn't that vital and each tempo expended on the kingside equates to one less pawn advancement on the queenside. It's all about the relative values of the two sides' connected passed pawns. In contrast to endgames of other types, in rook endings it's generally better to have extra centre pawns rather than outside ones. In king and pawn endings an enemy outside passed pawn must be halted by sending the defending king offside. If a defending rook can get behind a passed pawn in a rook and pawn situation then it is the attacker's king that must travel to the outside to try and aid its promotion.

Here I was expecting 35 b4. I can't say for sure that Black is winning but one possibility might be 35...♔d7 36 ♖b1 e5 37 a4 d4 38 a5 d3 39 ♔h2 (Or 39 ♔g1 d2 with ...♖c1 next up.) 39...e4 40 a6 ♔c7 41 ♖a1 ♔b8 4... b5 e3 43 b6 ♖c8 and unlike White, Black has the enemy passed pawns under control.

In fact my opponent played the more cautious 35 ♖f2 and in observing the game continuation you can compare the relative importance of the two pawn-pairs:

35...♔d7 36 g4 e5 37 ♔g2 ♔e6

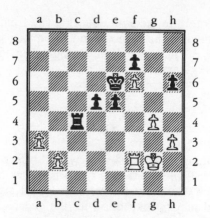

38 ♔g3 d4 39 h4 ♖c8 40 g5 hxg5 41 hxg5 ♖g8 42 ♔g4 e4 43 ♔f4 e3 44 ♖g2 ♔d5 45 ♔f3 ♖e8 (Black's next phase is all about achieving ...d3. Note how White is never allowed the opportunity to arrange a blockade.) 46 ♔e2 ♔c4 47 ♖g4 ♖h8 48 g6 (If White attempted to prevent the forthcoming check with 48 ♖g2 then 48 ...♖h3 would ensure that ...d3+ soon follows.) 48...♖h2+ 49 ♔f1 ♖f2+ 50 ♔g1 (Or 50 ♔e1 fxg6 51 ♖xg6 when each of 51...♔d3, 51...d3 and 51...♖xb2 are more than adequate for the win.) 50...fxg6 51 ♖xg6 ♖f5 52 f7 ♖xf7 0-1

Hence 5 points for **B**.

Q5

I'm going to give a point to C and those who presumably observed the following variation:

1 ♘g6+ fxg6 2 b8=♕+ ♔h7 3 ♕h8+! ♔xh8 4 ♕e8+ ♔h7 5 ♕h8+! ♔xh8

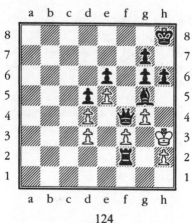

124

Yes and a very nice stalemate. Unfortunately instead Black has:

1...♔h7! as after 2 ♘xf4 (There is nothing after 2 ♘f8+ ♔g8) 2...♗xf4 there is no way to stop ...♖xh2 mate e.g. 3 g5 h5 4 g6+ ♔h6.

As it's clear that the knight doesn't have to be taken, 1 b8=♕+ ♔h7 is no improvement on these variations. 5 points for **E**.

Q6

If you'd not seen it, your decision might have been influenced by the variation:

13 exf6 hxg5?? (but other moves leave White a piece for the odd pawn up) 14 ♕xe6+!!

A really nice move and in the game Tunik-J.Geller, Russian Cup 2001, obviously not fancying the idea of 14...fxe6 15 ♗g6 mate, Black promptly resigned.

C is of course complete rubbish and I prefer Black after 1 ♗xf6 gxf6. As White is probably better after 1 ♗h4 ♗xf3 (watch out for the same 13...g5 14 exf6 gxh4 15 ♕xe6+!! trick again) 14 gxf3 ♘xe5 15 ♕xe5 ♗d6, I am left with little option but to merely give the basic 5 points for **A**.

Q7

In the game Gyimesi-Miladinovic, Malta Open 2000, from our quiz position the game continued:

10 &c4 0-0-0 11 &xd5 (I'm sure it pained White to do this but presumably he didn't want to drop a pawn and 11 fxe6 ♕xe6+ 12 ♔d1 feels unpleasant.) 11...♕xd5 (Either recapture would have led to a Black advantage but, although arguably the edge was bigger after 11...exd5, this way Black can play to win with no risk whatsoever.) 12 ♕xd5 ♖xd5 13 fxe6 fxe6 14 &c3 b5!? 15 0-0-0 b4 16 &d2 ♘xd4 17 ♘xd4 ♖xd4 18 ♖he1 &c5 19 ♖xe6 ♖c4+ 20 ♔b1 &xf2 21 ♖c1 ♖xc1+ 22 ♔xc1 &c5 23 ♖e5 &d6 24 ♖a5 ♖f8 25 &e3 &xh2 26 ♖xa7 ♖f1+ 27 ♔d2 ♖f6 28 ♖a8+ ♔b7 29 ♖a7+ ♔c8 30 ♖a8+ ♔d7 31 g4 &f4 32 ♔d3 &xe3 33 ♔xe3 ♖e6+ 34 ♔f3 ♔d6 35 a3 ♔c5 36 axb4+ ♔xb4 37 ♖a7 ♖c6 38 ♔f4 ♔c5 39 ♔e5 ♔b6 40 ♖a3 ♖c5+ 41 ♔e6 ♖b5 42 ♖h3 h6 43 ♔f7 ♖g5 44 ♖b3+ ♔c6 45 ♖b4 ♔d6 46 ♖c4 c6 47 ♖a4 ♔c7 48 ♖b4 h5 49 gxh5 ♖xh5 50 ♖g4 ♖b5 0-1

Possibly critical to a variation in the Chigorin Defence, after studying it for a while (i.e. with the above game in mind) I commented that it looks to me as though 10 ♕xb7!? is now the only way for White to strive for the advantage. He shouldn't get his queen trapped but after 10...♖b8 11 ♕a6 Black clearly has some play for the pawn. However as 11...♖xb2?! 12 &b5! is a problem, unless he wants to take on f5 instead, it may have to remain as a genuine sacrifice.

I'm sorry, this was sort of a tough question. Still 5 points for **B** (and 2 points for the more cautious D).

Q8

The bemusing 1 ♔d6 is of course poppycock but the others all need to be considered in order to understand the subtlety of the solution:

a) 1 ♔f5? ♔g2 2 h4 (the only hope as the f2-pawn is doomed and the arrival of a new black queen inevitable) 2...♔xf2 3 h5 ♔e3 4 h6 f2 5 h7 f1=♕+ (i.e. queening with check) 6 ♔g6 ♕f8 and White's pawn is stopped and easily rounded up.

b) 1 ♔e5? ♔g2 2 h4 ♔xf2 3 h5 ♔e3 4 h6 f2 5 h7 f1=♕ (It's not check this time but there's trouble brewing!) 6 h8=♕ ♕a1+!

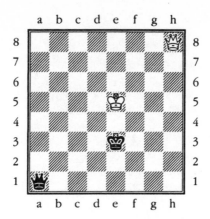

which is of course a rather nifty skewer! Whilst the white king needs to backtrack somehow, the key revolves around finding it a 'safe' path. One exists in:

c) 1 ♔d5! ♚g2 (Note that Black can't afford to be too clever as White's last subtle move still kept him within touching distance of Black's f3-pawn. Hence 1...♚xh2?? 2 ♔e4 ♚g2 3 ♔e3 is suddenly losing for Black who must of course budge from his current position.) 2 h4 ♚xf2 3 h5 ♚e3 4 h6 f2 5 h7 f1=♕ 6 h8=♕. As Black has no winning sequence it's a draw.

5 points for **B**.

Q9

We're back to that favourite Tebb-Ward, British Championship 1998, encounter of mine again, only this time a possible side variation.

Ruling out D, a trade of queens would clearly favour White who would have a well-placed bishop for a knight as well as domination of the d-file.

I'm going to award a sympathy 1 point for E although you will have to accept that (cheating in postal games aside) computers can't play the game for you! Getting to the nitty gritty then after 21...♘c3+ we have:

a) 22 bxc3? bxc3+ 23 ♔a1

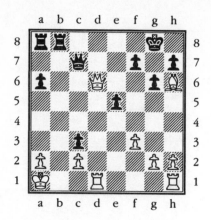

23...♖b1+!! 24 ♔xb1 (well obviously 24 ♖xb1 is better but then the queen is no longer protected) 24...♕b7+ 25 ♔a1 ♕b2 mate.

b) Not all forced but 22 ♔c1 ♘xa2+ 23 ♔b1 ♘c3+ 24 ♔c1 ♕a5 25 ♕f6 ♕a1+ 26 ♔d2 ♖d8+ 27 ♔e3 ♕c1+!! 28 ♖xc1 ♘d5+ 29 ♔e4 ♘xf6+ 30 ♔xe5 ♖d5+ 31 ♔xf6 ♖e8 with mate inevitable is an amusing variation that I hadn't noticed before doing this book. Black is better in this variant.

c) 22 ♔a1! ♕a5 23 bxc3 b3 24 cxb3 ♕xc3+ 25 ♔b1 ♖xb3+ 26 axb3 ♕xb3+ 27 ♔a1 ♕c3+ 28 ♔a2 ♕c2+ 29 ♔a3 ♕c3+ 30 ♔a4 ♕c4+ 31 ♕b4 ♕a2+ 32 ♕a3 ♕c4+. A fairly forcing sequence that has ended in a perpetual check.

5 points for **B**.

Q10

It's quite possible that you might have got a bit confused by this question and were maybe even doubting that the position was as I intended it. Yes A and B are obviously ridiculous and the answer for 5 points is **E**:

1 exd7 (it looks as though things are straightforward but Black has an ingenious saving trick) 1...♗b5! 2 d8=♕ (One key point is that after 2 ♔xb5 c6+ the black monarch can reach the pawn: 3 ♔a5 ♔c7 4 ♔a6 ♔xd7 5 ♔xa7 ♔d6 6 ♔b6 ♔d5 7 ♔c7 ♔c4 8 ♔xc6 ♔xb4) 2...a6!

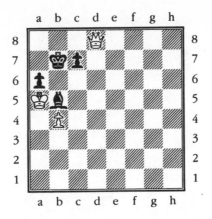

It's nothing to do with stalemate but here the white king is completely stuck. All Black need move is his king and as 3 ♕d5+ ♚b8 4 ♕e4 ♚a7 5 ♕e7 ♚b8 shows, an adequate fortress has been erected.

Q11

No doubt Keith will want to forget the miniature Nataf-Arkell, French Team Championship 2001. Actually I believe that White is better after each of the suggestions but I'll award 2 points each for D and E. For 5 points you can't argue with C and the game selection of:

14 ♕a3! (preventing Black from castling whilst of course threatening mate on e7) 14...♗f8 15 ♕b3 ♗g7 16 ♘g5

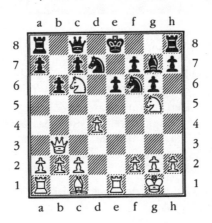

Here the white knights are extremely menacing and the presence of the white rook and queen too provoked a resignation here. There are sacrifices on e6 and f7 to consider and neither 16...♘b8 17 ♘xe6 fxe6 18 ♖xe6+ ♔f8 19 ♗h6 nor 16...♘f8 17 ♘e5 bear thinking about.

Q12

This ending occurred in the game Fischer-Keres, Zurich 1959, where in order to win, the American superstar merely had to be sure not to allow Black to concede his bishop for the f-pawn:

1 h6+ ♔h8 (Instead 1...♔f7 2 ♗h5+ ♔g8 3 ♗g6 would reach the same position but via a different route.) 2 ♗f5 ♗d5 3 ♗g6 ♗e6 4 ♔f6 ♗c4 5 ♔g5 ♗e6 6 ♗h5 ♔h7 7 ♗g4! ♗c4 (Of course 7...♗xg4 8 ♔xg4 ♔xh6 9 ♔f5+ is a won king and pawn ending.) 8 f5 ♗f7 9 ♗h5 ♗c4 10 ♗g6+ ♔g8 11 f6

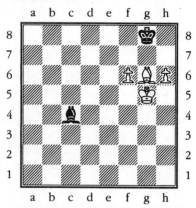

It was at this stage of the game that Black actually resigned, presumably because he didn't fancy hanging around for the likes of 11...♗b3 12 ♔f4 ♔h8 (Leaving the king on g8 hands White a simple plan on a plate, e.g. 12...♗a2 13 ♔e5 ♗b3 14 ♔d6 ♗a2 15 ♔e7 ♗b3 16 ♗f5 with ♗e6 coming next.) 13 ♔e5 ♗c4 14 ♔d6 ♗b3 15 ♔e7 ♗c4 16 ♗f7. The preparatory work has been done and now White sets about the serious (but not difficult) business of squeezing the defending bishop off of the key diagonal. 16...♗d3 17 ♗e8! ♗c4 18 ♗d7 ♗g8 19 ♗e6 ♗h7 20 f7. And no it's not stalemate!

D and particularly E are ridiculous whilst B confuses bishops with rooks. It's 5 points for **A**.

Q13

Really 1...♕xf1? 2 ♕xf1 ♖xf1 should be a lost rook and pawn ending e.g. 3 ♖xb5 d3 4 ♖d5 ♖b1 5 ♖xd3 ♖xb2 6 ♖d8+ ♔g7 7 ♖d7+ ♔g8 8 ♖xa7 ♖xh2 9 ♖b7 when the a-pawn would promote.

Nothing comes of 1...h6+ 2 ♔xh6 ♕xh2+ (or 2...♖f6+ 3 ♔g5) 3 ♖h5 but rather stunning is 1...♖g8+! 2 ♔h6 (obviously preferable to 2 ♔h4 ♕xh2 mate) 2...♕xh2+ 3 ♖h5 ♕d2+!!

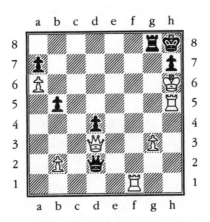

A delightful theme. With this queen sacrifice Black lures away its opposite number so that after 4 ♕xd2 (Lasting longer but hopeless is 4 ♖f4 ♕xd3.) the path is clear for 4...♖g6 mate.

5 points for **C** and out of the kindness of my heart I'll give 1 point to **D** anyway!

Q14

First off I believe that 15...♘xf2 is a mistake as 16 ♖xf2 ♕g3 17 ♗d4 ♖d8 18 ♗xc5 ♖xd1+ 19 ♖xd1 leaves White with too many pieces for the queen. Instead both 15...♗xf3 16 hxg4 ♖d8 17 ♕c2 ♗c6 and simply 15...♖d8 are fine for Black but my Wood Green teammate in the 4NCL (Hennigan-Short, Birmingham 2001) had a more adventurous continuation in mind:

15...h5! (Demonstrating why there is no need to retreat the knight and, by the way, 11...♕g3?? just blunders a piece.) 16 hxg4 ♗xf3 (16...hxg4? is a mistake as the queen sacrifice after 17 ♗e5! gxf3 18

♗xc7 fxg2 fails in view of 19 ♗f3 or 19 ♗h5.) 17 g5 (White is naturally eager to keep the h-file closed for reasons well observed after 17 ♗xf3? hxg4. Mate is threatened on h2 and to make matters worse (as in the game) 18 ♖e1 runs into 18...♕g3!! making the most of the pinned f2-pawn and causing significant problems there as well.) 17...♖d8 18 ♕c2 ♗c6 19 ♖ad1 ♖xd1 20 ♕xd1 h4 (Determined to get his rook in on the action Black has 21...h3 in mind when, as things stand, 22 g3 would allow either 22...h2 or 22...♕g3, both mate!) 21 ♗f3 (It's no great surprise then that White contests at least one critical diagonal but Black is not put off.) 21...h3 22 ♗xc6+ bxc6 (22...♕xc6 also looks very reasonable although then White has both 23 ♕g4 and the bale out 23 ♕f3 as defensive resources.) 23 ♗xg7?! (23 ♕g4 would have offered a bit more resistance although it's really not a nice position to have to defend.) 23...hxg2 24 ♗xh8 ♕g3!!

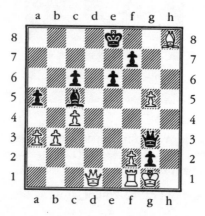

(A really cool move. One threat is 25...gxf1=♕+ 26 ♔xf1 ♕xf2 mate) 25 ♗d4 ♕h3 (And this is the other! The only way to prevent 26...♕h1 mate is by advancing the f-pawn but then it's mate in two via 26...♗xd4+.) 0-1

White's resignation here influences my decision of 5 points for **D**. The wording is a bit of an exaggeration but I'll award 2 points if you chose C instead.

Q15

This may seem really unfair but alas the answer for 5 points is **E**. Hopefully you will have observed that D is irrelevant to say the least and that C could be ruled out because the long-range bishop is not easily trapped!

Vital to the defence is that the bishop remains available to check the king if it comes to either b3 (e.g. 1...♔b3 2 ♗e6+) or d3.

Also important to note is that although 1...c2 2 ♗xc2 ♔c3 3 ♗a4 ♖g1+ 4 ♗d1 ♖h1 is a successful pawn sacrifice, far stronger is 2 ♔b2!

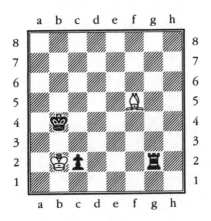

Above White is in no hurry to take the pawn and after 2...c1=♕+ 3 ♔xc1 ♔c3, White can prevent 4...♖g1 mate by moving his king.

Q16

All of the suggestions may look fairly plausible until you notice that 30...exd3?? simply drops a piece after 31 ♖xe8+ ♘xe8 32 ♗xd5. White is also better after 30...e3 31 ♔h1! as 31...exf2 32 ♖xe8+ ♘xe8 33 ♗xd5 is the same story. I'm going to award 2 points each for A and B but as my fellow countryman superbly demonstrated, C strikes gold (5 points):

Gelfand-Adams, Wijk aan Zee 2002, continued 30...♖xf2!! 31 ♖xf2 ♘f4.

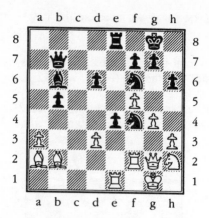

(Here Black has sacrificed a rook but his remaining pieces are fantastic. In particular there is an excellent pin on the b6-g1 diagonal and the f4-knight is awesome.)

32 ♕g3 (Amazingly 32 ♕f1 exd3! 33 ♖xe8+ ♘xe8 is crushing for Black in view of 34...♘e2+. Great stuff!) 32...♗xf2+ 33 ♔xf2 (Forced as 33 ♕xf2 ♘xh3+ is a simple fork) 33...♘xd3+ 34 ♔f1 ♘xb2 35 h4 (Black has emerged a couple of very handy pawns up.) 35...♕d7 36 ♔g2 ♘d3 37 ♖f1 e3 38 g5 hxg5 39 hxg5 ♘h5. With ...e2 imminent White resigned.

Q17

Option E is hardly answering the question but as it's wrong anyway I don't really need to fret about its validity. From our quiz position the game Ward-Knott, 4NCL, Birmingham 2001, saw:

32...♖b8? 33 ♗xc6 ♖xb1 34 d7 ♖d1 35 ♔e2

Quite a surprising situation, here the black rook is unable to safely remain on the d-file where it is of course required to monitor White's d-pawn. Hence 35...♗xe5 36 fxe5 ♖xd7 37 ♗xd7 f6 38 e6 ♔f8 39 ♔d3 ♔e7 40 ♔c4 ♔d6 41 ♗c8 h5 42 e7 ♔xe7 43 ♔xc5 ♔d8 44 ♗e6 1-0

As it looks as though 33 d7 ♗xe5 (or 33...♗xb5 34 ♗xb8 ♗xd7 35 ♗xa7 c4 36 ♗d4) 34 ♗xc6 is also winning, the answer for 5 points is **A**. Black should have played 32...♗xb5 with reasonable drawing chances.

Q18

Actually this was quite a sneaky one (nothing new there then!). Very instructive, though it should be apparent that both 1 a3 and 1 ♔c7 enable Black to promote easily via either 1...a4 or 1...h4. Correct play is:

1 a4 ♔b4 (White promotes first after the likes of 1...f4 2 a5 h4 3 a6 h3 4 gxh3 f3 5 a7)

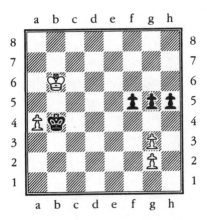

2 ♔b6! (Upon 2 ♔c6 f4 3 gxf4 gxf4 4 ♔d5 it is clear that White's king is too slow in returning after 4...f3! 5 gxf3 h4 as his own f-pawn obstructs the vital retreating diagonal.) Superbly demonstrating the flexibility of the king, the text is particularly accurate as White buys himself a critical tempo. As before, now 2...f4 would see White promote first and hence: 2...♔xa4 3 ♔c5 ♔b3! (Now Black is the one who must be precise in order to draw.

Note 3...h4? 4 gxh4 gxh4 5 ♔d4 f4 6 ♔e4 would leave his king well off the pace.) 4 ♔d4 ♔c2 5 ♔e5 ♔d3 6 ♔xf5 ♔e3 7 ♔xg5 (or 7 g4 hxg4 8 ♔xg4 ♔f2) 7...♔f2 8 ♔xh5 ♔xg3 and the remaining pawn will drop.

It should be a draw with 1 a4 and therefore it's 5 points for **B**.

Q19

Did my wording deceive you into avoiding **E** (sorry about that!) or did you simply take the cop-out option? Either way it nets 5 points. It was a very tough question as it is a difficult position upon which no doubt more light will be shed in the future.

Not long ago I annotated the game Rogovski-Golubev, Ukraine Championship 2001, on my www.chesspublishing Dragon website which continued: 15...♗f5 16 g4 (If he didn't know otherwise, White could be forgiven for believing that he is winning at this juncture. As detailed in my book *Winning With The Dragon (1)* several years ago, Black however has a neat trick at his disposal.) 16...f6!

(The point is that after 17 gxf5 g5, the white queen is trapped and will be won by ...♘f7. Meanwhile Black can still meet 17 hxg6 with 17...♗xg6.) 17 ♕f4 (The most obvious response although 17 ♕d2 is also interesting. Though not forced Black can then grab another pawn with 17...♘xf3 18 ♕f4 ♖ab8 with threats for both sides.) 17...♖ab8! (The only other game in this variation I could find was 17...♗d7 18 hxg6 ♘xg6 19 ♕h6 ♖f7 20 ♗d3 ♘f8 21 ♖de1 ♖b8 22 b3 ♕b4 23 ♘e2 a5 24 ♘f4 a4 25 ♘g6 ♘xg6 26 ♗xg6 ♖g7 27 ♗xh7+ ♔f7 28 ♔b1 axb3 29 cxb3 ♕a3 30 ♖e2 d4 31 ♗d3 ♖xb3+ 32 axb3 ♕xb3+ 33 ♔c1 ♕c3+ 34 ♗c2 d3 35 ♖xe7+ ♔xe7 36 ♕xg7+ ♔d6 37 ♖h2 ♕a1+ 38 ♗b1 ♕c3+ 39 ♔d1 ♕b3+ 40 ♗c2 dxc2+ 41 ♖xc2 ♕xf3+ 42 ♔c1 ♕a3+ 43 ♔d2 ♕b4+ 44 ♔c1 ♕a3+ ½-½ Schmitt-Werner, Germany 1993. The text looks more exciting!) 18 b3 (18 ♘a4 ♕b4!? 19 ♖d4! ♕e1+ 20 ♖d1 ♖b4 (Of course Black could repeat with 20...♕b4) 21 ♖xe1 ♖xf4 22 gxf5 ♖xa4 23 hxg6 hxg6 24 fxg6 ♖xa2 is a good ending for Black whilst 18 gxf5? ♕xb2+ 19 ♔d2 ♖b4! 20 ♕g3 ♖d4+ is curtains.) 18...g5! (An ambitious continuation. Instead both 18...♗d7 19 hxg6 ♘xg6 20 ♕h6 ♖f7 21 ♗d3 ♖g7 22 ♗xg6 hxg6 23 ♘a4 ♕b4 24 ♘c5! and 18...♕a5?! 19 gxf5! ♕xc3 20 hxg6 look a little worrying for Black.) 19 ♕xf5 ♕e3+ 20 ♔b2 ♖f7! (Heralding the threat of 21...e6! 22.♕xe6 ♘c4+.) 21 ♗d3 (Observe 21 ♖d3 ♘c4+! 22 ♔b1 ♕e1+! 23 ♘d1 [or 23 ♖d1 ♕xc3] 23...e6 winning heavy material.) 21...e6 (This pawn is out of bounds because of a knight check winning the white queen.) 22 ♖he1 ♕xe1 23 ♕xh7+ ♖xh7 24 ♗xh7+ ♔xh7 25 ♖xe1 (After all that an endgame is reached in which Black holds the upper hand because of his more dangerous-looking pawns.) 25...♖b4 26 ♘e2 ♘xf3 27 ♖f1 ♖xg4 (27...♘e5 28 ♖xf6 ♖e4 still leaves Black on top as the rook indirectly defends the e-pawn thanks to a knight check again whilst the g4-pawn is still hanging. The game continuation looks fun but is objectively not best.) 28 ♖xf3 f5 29 ♖e3 (After the active looking 29 ♖c3? ♖e4! 30 ♘g3 ♖e1 31 ♖xc6 f4, White's knight is lost.) 29...f4 30 ♘xf4! (30 ♖xe6 f3 31 ♘c1 f2 32 ♖f6 ♖f4 is what Black probably had in mind but White finds an accurate defence.) 30...♖xf4! 31 ♖xe6 ♖f7 (Angling to manoeuvre the rook behind the dangerous passed g-pawn. Now White hasn't enough time to capture on c6.) 32 ♔c3 g4 33 ♔d3! g3 (Upon 33...♖g7?! 34 ♔e2 g3 35 ♔f1 g2+ 36 ♔g1 the white rook would be free to cause some damage.) 34 ♖g6 ♖g7 35 ♖xg7+ ♔xg7 36 ♔e3 ♔h6 37 ♔f3 ♔xh5 38 ♔xg3 ♔g5 ½-½

I'm not sure if you ploughed through all that or not but if you did you'll appreciate that it's like I said; complicated stuff!

Q20

Those who have read the first volume of *Chess Choice Challenge* will be used to this sort of question and will have hopefully taken on board the examples I gave in king and queen vs king and pawn on the 7th rank situations. Cutting a long story short, the closer the attacking king is to the 7th rank pawn the more chance of winning he has. Nevertheless provided it is not an a-, c-, f- or h-pawn (i.e. 50% of the time!) the distance away is irrelevant as the queen can force the king in front of the pawn to buy time to return the monarch to active duty.

Our quiz position is won as demonstrated by:

1 ♕a2 ♚c3 2 ♕a1+ ♚d2 (Obviously Black cannot allow the white queen to occupy the c1-square.) 3 ♕b2 (Again pinning the pawn.) 3...♚d1 4 ♔f3

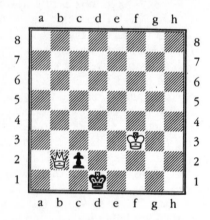

4...♚d2 (The white king is clearly close enough to have an influence. This critical point is illustrated by the variation 4...c1=♕ 5 ♕e2 mate. Also note that as in our main line, 4...c1=♘ 5 ♔e3 is hopeless.) 5 ♔e4 ♚d1 6 ♔d3 c1=♘+ (Again, of course, a queen promotion would allow 7 ♕e2 mate.) 7 ♔e3 winning quickly.

I'm going to give a point to B (failing only because the attacking king is close enough) and a point for D (alas his king won't be allowed around to that side of the pawn). The 5 points however go to the selection of E.

Test Four: Answers

Q1

Although you may be disappointed with the lack of realism associated with this problem, I just couldn't resist including it. If you solved it (the answer isn't E!) then I hope you had fun in doing so and if not then be amazed by the following:

1 ♘b8+ ♗xb8 (Forced in view of 1...♔xc7 2 ♖d7+ ♔xb8 3 ♖xb7+ ♔a8 4 ♖xe7+ ♔b8 5 ♖b7+ ♔a8 6 ♖xb6+ ♗d5 7 ♗xd5 mate.) 2 cxb8=♘+ ♔c7 3 ♘a6+ bxa6 (Also necessary as 3...♔c6 4 ♘xb4+ ♔c7 5 ♖d7+ ♔b8 6 ♖xb7+ ♔a8 7 ♖xe7+ ♗d5 8 ♗xd5+ ♔b8 9 ♘a6 is another nice mate.) 4 ♖d7+ ♔b8 5 ♖b7+ ♔a8 6 ♖xe7+ (And so starts White's fun. Black could at any time interpose the bishop but that would merely transpose to our main line.) 6...♔b8 7 ♖b7+ (The good old 'rocker' checks in action. It was necessary to remove the e7-knight first as that could have blocked the key f3-a8 diagonal. White can't take the f7 yet as then his rook will be pinned to his king (I'm sure that Black's material advantage elsewhere hasn't escaped your attention!) and so now is the time to plough through the b-file.) 7...♔a8 8 ♖xb6+ ♔a7 9 ♖b7+ ♔a8 10 ♖xb5+ ♔a7 11 ♖b7+ ♔a8 12 ♖xb4+ ♔a7 13 ♖b7+ ♔a8 14 ♖xb3+ ♔a7 15 ♖b7+ ♖xb7 16 ♖xb7+ (Delightful! As if on as a substitute, the other rook is tagged into action.) 16...♔a8 17 ♖xf7+ ♔b8 18 ♖xf6

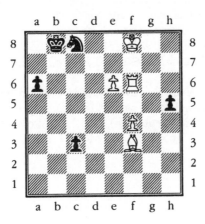

(I'm going to award 3 points for A if you didn't move any pieces from the start position and analyzing ahead concluded that Black could resign here. In fact there is still a bit more work to be done.) 18...c2 19 e7 ♘xe7 (19...c1=♕ 20 e8=♕ is hopeless for Black who doesn't come remotely close to a perpetual check.) 20 ♔xe7 c1=♕ 21 ♖b6+ ♔c7 (Walking back into the same old story via 21...♔a7 22 ♖b7+ ♔a8 23 ♖c7+ is no better.) 22 ♖c6+ ♕xc6 23 ♗xc6 ♔xc6 24 f5 h4 25 f6 h3 26 f7 h2 27 f8=♕ h1=♕ 28 ♕a8+.

Just the 28 moves then with the move finally convincing Black to resign given in C (a hard earned 5 points).

What can I say? It's fantastic and a brilliant concoction by Luke McShane and Jon Speelman who deserve our appreciation for pure entertainment value.

Q2

Checking out some options we have:

a) 1 ♔d1 ♔c3 2 ♔c1 ♗d5 3 ♔b1 ♗e4 which is trivial.

b) 1 e4 ♔c3 2 e5 ♗e6 3 ♔b1 ♗f5 4 ♔c1 ♗xc2 5 e6 b3 6 e7 b2 mate. i.e. not much different.

c) 1 ♔b2 ♗b3!! (an important idea) 2 cxb3+ (If 2 e4 then the bishop escapes via 2...♗a4 and capturing the e-pawn with the king will be the first phase of an easy winning task.) 2...♔d3 (Now White will lose both pawns and, as the black king will obviously capture the b-pawn on the 6th rank, he will certainly win.) 3 e4 ♔xe4 4 ♔c2 ♔e3 5 ♔c1 ♔d3 6 ♔b2 ♔d2 7 ♔b1 ♔c3 8 ♔a2 ♔c2 9 ♔a1 ♔xb3 10 ♔b1 ♔a3 11 ♔a1 b3 12 ♔b1 b2 13 ♔c2 ♔a2.

d) 1 ♔d2! ♔c5 (Now 1...♗b3 2 cxb3+ ♔xb3 3 e4 ♔a2 [or 3...♔c4 4 ♔c2 ♔d4 5 ♔b3 ♔xe4 6 ♔xb4] 8 e5 is only a draw as both sides promote pawns simultaneously.) 2 c3 b3 3 ♔c1 ♔c4 4 ♔b2 ♔d3 5 e4 ♔xe4 6 c4 ♔d4 7 c5 ♔xc5 8 ♔a1 ♔b4 9 ♔b2 ♔c4 10 ♔a1

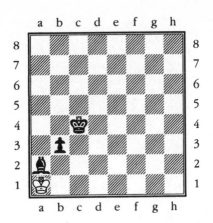

Yes, here is one of those rare exceptions where, despite his significant material plus, the attacker can make no progress. 5 points for **B** but I'll give 1 point for A as well.

Q3

This one is fairly straightforward. The only way for White to win is with 1 ♔a4 ♚b6 2 ♔b4 ♚c6 3 ♔c4 ♚d6 4 ♔d4 ♚e6 5 ♔e4 ♚f6 (or 5...g3 6 fxg3 ♚f6 7 ♔f4 ♚g6 8 ♔g4 ♚h6 9 ♔f5 etc.) 6 ♔f4 ♚f7 7 ♔xg4 ♚g6 8 ♔f4 ♚f6 as the critically available 9 f3 returns him the opposition.

5 points for **C**.

Q4

In Barsov-Zhang Zhong, Hastings Premier 2001, White kicked off his tournament nicely by demolishing the top seed. He chose:

29 ♖f6+!!

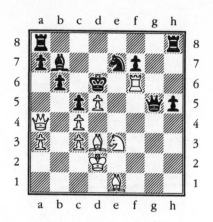

(Extremely visual and note 29 ♗g3+?! ♕xg3 30 ♖f6+ ♚c7 31 d6+ ♕xd6! would clearly have nothing like the same impact.) 29...♚e5 (The point is that 29...♕xf6 suffers heavily at the hands of 30 ♗g3+ and 29...♚c7 30 d6+ ♚c8 31 dxe7 is of course no better. Although the rook is *en prise*, all of a sudden a white pawn is on the verge of promotion!) 30 ♖f3 (Bringing the concept of ♗g3+ into play.) 30...f5 31 ♗xf5! ♖hd8 3... ♗g3+ ♚f6 33 ♗c8+ (33 ♗e6+ ♚g7 34 ♖f7+ ♚h8 35 ♗f4 with 36 ♗e5+ in mind would have been a cleaner finish but from here on in there was only going to be one winner.) 33...♚g7 34 ♗xb7 ♖f8 35 ♗f4 ♖xf4 36 ♖xf4 ♖d8 37 ♖f2 ♘g6 38 ♖g2 ♕f4 39 ♕c2 ♖d6 40 ♕f5 1-0

5 points for **D**.

Q5

Regarding E, I'm afraid that you should always take the time control into consideration when making other arrangements. A little sympathy for this selection though as I know many a GM who has ended up missing his travel home because of a long game. Nevertheless no points and none also for D. It is unethical to play on in a completely lost position of which this is certainly NOT.

Although Black did resign in Emms-Degraeve, Mondariz 2000, the Frenchman could only look on in disbelief as their post mortem analysis uncovered:

56...c2 57 g6 a2 58 g7 ♖a8! 59 ♖a1

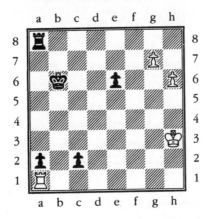

(Black is the one with an extra pawn but with a draw very likely after 59 h7 a1=♕ 60 ♖xa1 ♖xa1 61 h8=♕ ♖h1+ 62 ♔g3 ♖xh8 63 gxh8=♕ c1=♕) 59...♖c8! (The big point and much preferable to 59...c1=♕? 60 ♖xc1 a1=♕ 61 ♖xa1 ♖xa1 62 g8=♕ ♖h1+ 63 ♔g2) 60 ♖c1 (60 h7 c1=♕ 61 ♖xc1 ♖xc1 62 h8=♕ ♖h1+ 63 ♔g2 a1=♕ 64 ♕b8+ ♔c5 65 ♕c7+ ♔d5 66 ♕b7+ ♔c5 67 ♕c7+ is also a draw as White can't afford to take a time out to promote another queen.) 60...♖a8. I will award 2 points for A but as it is clear that this game should end in a draw by repetition, it's 5 points for C.

Q6

With White to play we have:

1 ♘h2! ♔b8 (1...♔c8 2 ♔c6 ♔b8 3 ♔b6 would merely transpose whilst the super finesse 1...♔d8 is hardly applicable. Aside from the fact that 2 ♔b6 would obtain the diagonal opposition, I think that 2 a7 would suffice!) 2 ♔b6 ♔a8 3 ♘g4 ♔b8 4 a7+ ♔a8 5 ♘f6 h2 6 ♘d5 h1=♕ 7 ♘c7 mate!

143

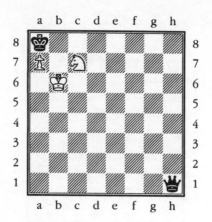

However with Black to play:

1...♚b8 2 ♚b6 (Important is 2 ♚c6 ♚a7! 3 ♚b5 ♚b8!) 2...♚a8 3 ♘h2 (3 ♘f6 h2 6 ♘d5 h1=♕ 7 ♘c7+ ♚b8 8 a7+ ♚c8 9 a8=♕+ ♕xa8 10 ♘xa8 also fails this time.) 3...♚b8 4 a7+ ♚a8 5 ♘g4 h2 and the knight is well off the pace. As this is only a draw it's 5 points for **D** (but I'll give 1 point for E as you've understood that tempi are important).

Q7

With reference to A, the above position is a theoretical draw as the black king is 'safe' on b7 (i.e. not vulnerable to any ♖a8-a7 style skewer tricks). Readers of *Endgame Play* and probably *CCC1* would have known that as well as the tactic that my Wood Green team mate missed in the game Shirov-Morozevich, Astana 2001.

From our quiz position, best was 55...♖xh5!! in view of 56 ♖a5+ ♔b4

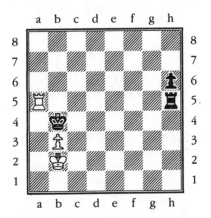

as 57 ♖xh5 is of course stalemate!

Instead Black lost painfully via 55...♔b4 56 ♖b6+ ♔c5 57 ♖xh6 ♔b4 58 ♔c2 ♖c3+ 59 ♔d2 ♖h3 60 ♖h8 ♔c5 61 ♔c2 ♔b5 62 ♔d2 ♔c6 63 h6 ♔b7 64 b4 ♔a7 65 ♔e2 ♖h4 66 ♔f3 ♖xb4 67 ♖g8 ♖h4 68 ♖g6 ♔b7 69 ♔g3 ♖h1 70 ♔f4 ♔c7 71 ♔f5 ♔d7 72 ♔f6 ♔e8 73 ♔g7 1-0

5 points for **E** but I'll give a generous 2 points for those of you that selected B.

Q8

Actually with the exception of E, I think that all of the suggestions are good. I'm going to trust your analysis and award 2 points each for A, B and C but the maximum 5 points for D. My reasoning is based on a entertaining tussle between two of England's players for the future:

Howell-McShane, Bunratty 2000: 1...♖xf2! 2 ♔xf2 ♖f8+ 3 ♔e2 ♕xb2+ 4 ♔d3 (If 4 ♕d2 then 4...♖f2+!) 4...♘b4+ 5 ♔d4 ♖f4+ 6 ♔c5 ♘a6+ 7 ♔d6 ♕b6+ 8 ♔e7 ♖f7+ 9 ♔e8 ♕c7

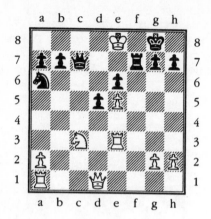

Having been a good sport about the whole combination, only now did David throw in the towel.

Q9

A for 5 points is the whole truth and nothing but the truth, e.g. 1 ♘c7 a5 2 ♘d5+ (After 2 ♘b5 a4 White is in 'zugzwang' as his king really doesn't want to move.) 2...♚b3 3 ♘xe3 a4

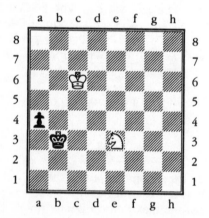

White has won Black's bishop but, barring one or two token attempts, there is no way to get at the black a-pawn: 4 ♘f1 (4 ♘f5 a3 5 ♘d4+ ♚b2 leaves White no better placed.) 4...a3 5 ♘d2+ ♚c2 6 ♘c4 a2 7 ♘e3+ ♚b3.

Q10

Though I often wonder about the usefulness of studies, many of them include instructive themes. Actually when broken down it really is simple, but this construction of Pervakov's is truly magnificent. By elimination:

a) 1 d4? f4 simply allows Black to queen first and with check.

b) 1 ♔xf5 b5 2 d4 b4 3 d5 b3 4 d6 b2 5 d7 b1=♛+ is the same story.

c) 1 ♔e5? b5 2 d4 b4 3 d5 b3 4 d6 b2 5 d7 b1=♛ 6 d8=♛ ♛e4+ 7 ♔d6 (or 7 ♔f6 ♛h4+) 7...♛d4+ 8 ♔c7 ♛xd8+ 9 ♔xd8 f4 also loses as the remaining pawn promotes.

Instead the stunning continuation that earns **E** 5 points is:

1 ♔g5! (Not the first move to enter one's head!) 1...b5 (White can also defend the crafty 1...♔b3 2 ♔xf5 ♔c3 with 3 ♔e5! [careful to ensure that the b-pawn doesn't queen with check] 3...b5 [or 3...♔xd3 4 ♔d5 when the king wins the b-pawn quickly] 4 d4 b4 5 d5 b3 6 d6 b2 7 d7 b1=♛ 8 d8=♛ and Black has no skewer.) 2 d4 b4 3 d5 ♔b5 4 d6! ♔c6 5 ♔xf5

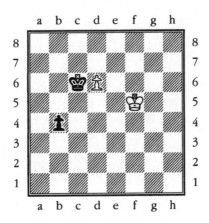

5...b3 (Or 5...♔xd6 6 ♔e4 ♔c5 7 ♔d3 with the white king able to hold.) 6 ♔e6 b2 7 d7 b1=♛ (Upon 7...♔c7 of course there is 8 ♔e7.) 8 d8=♛ and it's a draw!

I guess 'her' would be more applicable in this case (I must apologise to any female readers.) as in Xu Jun-Ivanchuk, Lucerne 1993, after 13 fxg7 Black uncorked the stunning 13...bxa1=♞!!

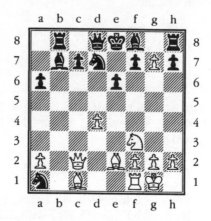

As well as being entertaining 13...bxa1=♕? 14 gxh8=♕ would certainly favour White who has by far the safer king. The text, though, sees the new knight hitting the white queen and thus provides Black with a material plus. The rest of the game was pretty convincing:

14 gxh8=♕ ♘xc2 15 ♗g5 ♗xf3 16 ♗xd8 ♗xe2 17 ♗xc7 ♖b7 18 ♗d6 ♗xf1 19 ♔xf1 ♖b6 20 ♗xf8 ♘xf8 21 g3 ♘b4 22 ♕e5 ♘d5 23 h4 ♘g6 24 ♕g7 h5 25 ♕g8+ ♔e7 26 ♕c8 ♘f8 27 a4 ♘d7 28 a5 ♖d6 29 ♕c4 ♔d8 30 ♕e2 ♘7f6 31 ♕c4 ♔d7 32 ♕c5 ♘e4 33 ♕a3 f5 34 ♔g2 ♖c6 35 ♕b2 ♔c8 36 ♕e2 ♘ef6 37 ♕b2 f4 38 gxf4 ♘xf4+ 39 ♔g3 ♘6d5 40 ♕d2 ♖c3+ 41 f3 ♔c7 42 ♕b2 ♖c6 43 ♕d2 ♔c8 44 ♕b2 ♖c7 45 ♔h2 ♖c4 46 ♕a3 ♖b4 47 ♕c1+ ♔b7 48 ♕d2 ♔c6 49 ♕c2+ ♔b5 50 ♕c5+ ♔a4 51 ♕c6+ ♔xa5 52 ♕c5+ ♖b5 53 ♕a3+ ♔b6 54 ♕d6+ ♔a7 55 ♕d7+ ♖b7-+ 56 ♕d6 ♖c7 57 ♔h1 a5 58 ♕a3 ♔a6 59 ♕b3 ♖c6 60 ♔h2 ♘b6 61 ♕e3 ♘fd5 62 ♕e2+ ♘c4 0-1.

Eliminating the other obvious blunders I'd have to deduce that **B** for 5 points is the correct answer.

Q12

Converting this endgame does require a bit of work but in accordance with **D** (5 points) White should get there in the end:

1 ♘h6 ♚e4 2 ♘f7 ♗b2 3 ♘d6+ ♚d5 4 ♘e8 ♗h8 5 ♔f7 ♚e5 6 ♘g7 ♚d6

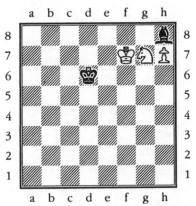

7 ♘h5! (I'm going to award 2 points to B because after 7 ♔g8 ♚e7 8 ♔xh8, instead of 8...♔f7 9 ♘e6, Black can indeed draw with 8...♔f8!) 7...♚d7 8 ♔f8 ♚d8 (or 8...♚e6 9 ♔g8 ♚e7 10 ♘g7) 9 ♘f4 ♚d7 10 ♔g8 ♚e8 (Both 10...♚e7 11 ♘g6+ and 10...♗b2 11 ♘h5, intending 12 ♘g7, spell the end.) 11 ♘e6 ♚e7 12 ♘g7 ♚f6 13 ♔xh8 ♚f7 14 ♘e6. The knight buys the king out of trouble and the pawn will promote.

Q13

Yes I know that this was a tough one and the game McShane-Rozentalis, North Sea Cup, Esbjerg 2001, actually ended with 25...♕f6 26 ♗d1 (and not 26 f4? ♘f3+ 27 gxf3 ♖xe3!) 26...♕f5 27 ♗c2 ♕f6 ½-½

Clearly 25...♗e4? 26 ♗xe4 ♕xe4 27 ♗xc5 is rubbish as is 25...♕xh3+?? 26 ♚xh3 whilst there is nothing after 21...♘f3+? 26 gxf3 ♕xf3 27 ♖g1. So checking out 25 ...♕f3!? we have:

26 gxf3 (and not 26 ♖g1 ♕xg2+! 27 ♖xg2 ♘f3+ 28 ♚h1 ♘xd2) 26...♘xf3+ 27 ♚g3 h4+

28 ♔g4! (Far preferable to 28 ♔f4 ♖f6+ 29 ♔g4 ♗c8+ 30 ♗f5 ♖xf5 31 ♗f4 ♘xe1 with some wicked material winning threats.) 28...f5+ 29 ♗xf5! (29 ♔f4 g5+ 30 ♔xf5 ♖e5+ 31 ♔g4 ♘h2+ 32 ♔h5 ♔g7, with both ...♖h8 and ...♗f3 in mind, is devastating e.g. 33 ♗f5 ♖xf5 34 ♗d4+ cxd4 35 ♕xd4+ ♖ee5) 29...gxf5+ 30 ♔f4 ♘xd2 31 ♗xd2. As this should be a drawing opposite-coloured bishop scenario it's **A** that deserves the 5 points.

Q14

I'm going to award 2 points for the sensible choice of A but it has to be 5 points for D:

Dreev-Balashov, Odessa 1989: 1 ♘xa5! (To get some serious action in the form of a passed pawn going on the queenside.) 1...bxa5 2 b6 ♘f8 (White has a serious space advantage and the black knights must scuttle around like rats!) 3 b7 ♘d7 4 h7 ♔g7

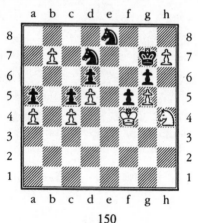

5 ♘xg6! ♚xh7 (else it would be the h-pawn queening) 6 ♘f8+! (A beautiful finish. White's remaining knight deflects its enemy counterpart from its vital role of controlling the passed pawn.) 1-0

Q15

1 point for B (as you got the right result) but for 5 points **E** is correct in view of:

1 ♗xb2 axb2

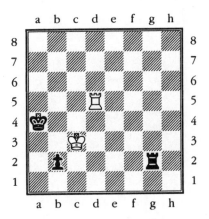

2 ♖d7! (After playing over the main line, compare the same variation with what would happen if the rook went to d8 instead. Note also that 2 ♖d1 ♚a3 is winning for Black e.g. 3 ♖d8 ♚a2 4 ♖a8+ ♚b1 5 ♖h8 ♖g3+ 6 ♚b4 ♖d3 7 ♖c8 ♖d7 8 ♖c6 ♖b7+ 9 ♚c3 ♚c1 when the pawn will shortly promote.) 2...b1=♘+ (White picks up the new queen after 2...b1=♛ 3 ♖a7+ ♚b5 4 ♖b7+.) 3 ♚c4 (The white king can't venture to the d-file yet in view of ...♖d2+.) 3...♖c2+ 4 ♚d5 ♖d2+ 5 ♚e6

With the rook on d7, the skewer isn't serious. Okay, if he wants to play on for a bit, Black shouldn't trade rooks yet but the ending is drawn with reasonable defence anyhow.

Q16

The occasion was Kasparov-Kramnik, Botvinnik Memorial match, Moscow 2001, in which Black actually did something different a move previously. The real game ended in a draw but far more entertaining is our quiz position with analysis as follows:

49 ♕c8+ (Only Black could play for the win after 49 ♘xh6+ gxh6 50 ♕c8+ ♔f7.) 49 ...♔h7 (The successful knight works overtime after 49...♔f7?? 50 ♘xe5+ ♔f6 51 ♘xd3 ♖xb1+ 52 ♘c1.) 50 ♘f6+!

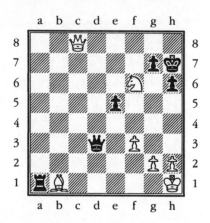

50...♔g6 (A key idea is 50...gxf6? 51 ♕d7+!! when White utilises the black queen to king pin to maximum benefit before he can get duffed up on the back rank.) 51 ♕e8+! ♔xf6 (As before, not 51...♔f5 52 ♕d7+, whilst the queen is again pinned after 51...♔g5 52 ♕xe5+ ♔g6 53 ♕xa1 and hence unavailable for ...♕f1 mate.) 52 ♕f8+ ♔e6 (Ill advised is 52...♔g5?? 53 ♕xg7+ ♔f4 54 ♕xh6+ ♔f5 55 g4 mate whilst 52...♔g6?? 53 ♕d6+ is the same old story.) 53 ♕e8+ ♔f6 54 ♕f8+ ♔e6. Yes it should by repetition and hence the 5 points go to **C**.

Q17

In Srebrnic-Zatonskih, European Team Championship, Leon 2001, Black found the stunning: 1...♗d4+!!

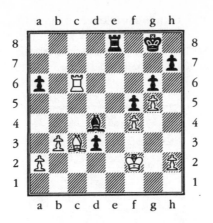

(Far superior to 1...♗xc3 2 ♖xc3 ♖e2+ [and not 2...d2? 3 ♖d3 ♖e4 4 ♔f3 which drops the pawn for nothing] 3 ♔g3 ♖xa2 4 ♖xd3 which should just be a draw.) 2 ♔f1 (The idea of course is that Black can't halt the passed pawn after 2 ♗xd4 d2 and there are no sneaky tricks for White on the 7th rank. Also after 2 ♔f3 ♖e3+ 3 ♔g2 ♖e2+ 4 ♔f3, Black can pin [and win!] the bishop [or the exchange] with ...♖c2, probably after driving away the enemy king further with 4...♖f2+.) 2...♗xc3 3 ♖xc3 d2 0-1

Yes, since it's suddenly all over as White can't stop ...♖e1+ and ...d1=♕, I have no option but to award 5 points for **C**.

Q18

Regarding option E, of course one should always pay heed to such principles but they are not the be all and end all. Each individual position should be taken on its own merits and besides as 'knights on the rim are dim' Black has transgressed too!

Indeed following the game Vera-Formanek, Andorra 1996, which started 1 d4 d5 2 c4 ♘c6 3 ♘c3 dxc4 4 d5 ♘a5, I believe that 5 ♕a4+! c6 6 b4 is probably the best way for White to play:

This encounter continued: 6...cxb3 7 axb3 e6 (Rather unattractive is 7...b6 8 dxc6 e5 9 e3 as White has both 10 b4 and 10 c7+ to deal with.) 8 ♗d2 (White's intention is to round up the errant knight but here 8 ♕xa5? ♕xa5 9 ♖xa5 runs into 9...♗b4.) 8...♘xb3 (Notching up more pawns for the piece as 8...exd5 9 ♕xa5 ♕xa5 10 ♖xa5 amounts to just two. The only way to preserve the offside knight is

153

with 8...b6 although then 9 dxc6 leaves a fantastic pawn and 9...♘e7 10 ♗g5! f6 11 ♖d1 ♘d5 12 e4 is very strong for White. Not only is the d5-knight attacked and pinned but 12...fxg5 is decisively met by 13 c7+ ♕d7 14 ♗b5) 9 ♕xb3 exd5 10 e4

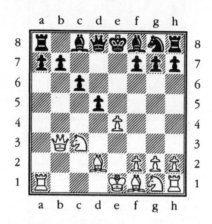

(Black has three connected passed pawns for the knight but typically pieces play a greater role than pawns in the opening/middlegame.) 10...d4 11 ♗c4! ♕d7 (Black can't take this knight as 11...dxc3? 12 ♗xf7+ ♔d7 13 ♗f4! leaves the black king caught in a fatal crossfire and 11...♕e7 12 ♘ce2 b5 13 ♗d3 ♘f6 14 ♘f3 is no better than the text as Black still can't get castled.) 12 ♘d5!? (12 ♘ce2 is a safer way to retain an advantage but, with all Black's army bar the queen on the back rank, White decides to go for it!) 12...b5 (Obviously the knight is safe on d5 for the time being because of ♗b5.) 13 ♗d3 ♗b7 (A different defence would be put up by 13...♖b8 but Black's big problem remains of developing his kingside.) 14 ♘f3 ♗d6 (14...cxd5? is still not possible because of 15 ♗xb5 ♗c6 16 ♘e5. White's next move really is effectively a sacrifice.) 15 0-0 cxd5 (Black takes up the challenge as 15...♘e7 16 ♘xe7 ♗xe7 17 ♗xb5! cxb5 18 ♘e5 leaves Black unable to protect both b5 and f7.) 16 ♗xb5 ♗c6 17 ♗xc6 ♕xc6 18 ♖fc1 (The piece count is now level but White has a significant lead in development.) 18...♕d7 19 ♕xd5 ♖d8 (This rook was attacked, leaving no time for the knight to come out.) 20 ♕xd4 ♗xh2+ (Upon 20...♘f6 each of 21 e5, 21 ♗a5 and 21 ♖xa7 would have left White in a winning position.) 21 ♔xh2 ♕xd4 (Black gets the queens off so that he won't be mated but his little liquidating combination has a flaw.) 22 ♘xd4 ♖xd4 23 ♗c3 1-0. Black will lose one of his rooks.

Theoretically it would appear that 6...b5 7 ♕xa5 ♕xa5 8 bxa5 b4 is the real position to debate. However, whichever way White opts to move his knight he still has the useful central break to chisel away at Black's pawns, so arguably both 9 ♘d1 cxd5 10 e4! and 9 ♘a4 cxd5 10 e4! favour White. As it's my decision I'm going to award 5 points for **D**.

Q19

After 21 ♗xh7+! ♚xh7 (Upon 21...♚h8 22 ♘xg5 g6 [or 22...f6 23 ♕h5 with an unstoppable mate in two via 24 ♗g6+] 23 ♕f3 ♕d8 [if 23...f6 then simply 24 ♗xg6] 24 ♕h3 ♚g7 then particularly jazzy is 25 ♗g8! ♖xg8 26 ♕h7+ ♚f8 27 ♕xf7 mate) 22 ♘xg5+

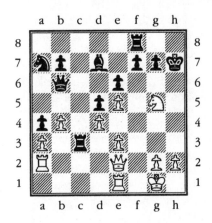

We have:

a) 22...♚g8 23 ♕h5 ♖fc8 24 ♕xf7+ ♚h8 25 ♕h5+ ♚g8 26 ♖f2 (spoilt for choice, 26 ♖f1 would also pen the enemy king in) with 27 ♕h7 unstoppable.

b) 22...♚h6 23 ♕g4! when Black must jettison too much material in order to avoid 24 ♕h4+ ♚g6 25 ♕h7+ ♚xg5 26 h4+ ♚g4 27 ♕xg7+ ♚xh4 28 g3+ ♚h3 29 ♖h2 mate.

c) 22...♚g6 23 ♕g4 f5 (No improvement is 23...f6 24 ♘xe6+ ♚f7 25 ♕xg7+ ♚xe6 26 ♕xf8 with a totally crushing position in view of 27 ♕xf6 or simply 27 ♖f2.) 24 ♕h4 ♕d8 (24...f4 25 ♕h7+ ♚xg5 26 ♕xg7+ ♚f5 27 ♕xf8+ ♚g6 may last more moves but that hardly makes it better!) 25 ♕h7+ ♚xg5 26 h4+ ♚g4. Now in the game Yemelin-Goric, Rijeka Open, Croatia 2001, Black resigned as he

155

didn't fancy hanging about for 27 ♕g6+ ♚xh4 28 g3+ ♚h3 29 ♖h2 mate.

With no points for anything else, it has to be the maximum 5 for **A**.

Q20

Regarding this informative study of Grigoriev, I believe that the following analysis should prove conclusive:

1...♚a5 (1...♚a6 2 b4 leaves White with the opposition and after 2...♚b6 3 ♚b8 ♚c6 4 ♚a7 ♚c7 5 ♚a6 ♚c6 6 ♚a5 he can guarantee picking up the remaining black pawn.) 2 ♚b8! (An important move as after 2 ♚b7? Black has 2...b4 because 3 c4 is of course stalemate.) 2...b4 (Again the last black pawn is lost after either 2...♚b6 3 b4 or 2...♚a6 3 ♚c7 ♚a5 4 ♚c6 ♚a6 5 b4.) 3 c4 ♚b6 (It may look as though the black monarch has its enemy number one trapped on the back rank but, as you will soon see, there is the 'square' of the supported passed c-pawn to take into consideration.) 4 ♚c8 ♚c6 5 ♚d8 ♚d6 6 ♚e8 ♚e6 7 ♚f8 ♚f6 8 ♚g8 ♚g6 9 ♚h8!

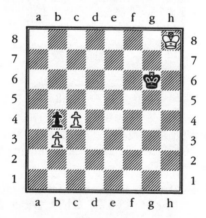

(The point. Now after 9...♚h6, Black would be unable to stop the c-pawn from promoting.) 9...♚f6 10 ♚h7 (The white king is slowly but surely returning to the sort of action where the concept of the opposition won't be so relevant.) 10...♚f7 11 ♚h6 ♚f6 12 ♚h5 ♚f5 13 ♚h4 ♚f4 (A very relevant feature throughout is that the likes of 13...♚e4 14 ♚g4 ♚d4 15 ♚f4 ♚c3 16 c5 ♚xb3 17 c6 ♚a2 18 c7 b3 19 c8=♕ b2 is lost because the 7th rank pawn is on a knight's file

156

e.g. 20 ♕a6+ ♚b3 21 ♕d3+ ♚a2 23 ♕c2 ♚a1 23 ♕a4+ ♚b1 24 ♚e3 ♚c1 25 ♕c4+ ♚b1 26 ♚d3 ♚a1 27 ♕a4+ ♚b1 28 ♚c3 ♚c1 29 ♕c2 mate.) 14 ♚h3! ♚f5 (Again the king cannot follow as on f3 it would be unable to monitor the progress of White's trump card on c4.) 15 ♚g3 ♚g5 16 ♚f3 ♚f5 17 ♚e3 ♚e5 18 ♚d3 ♚d6 19 ♚d4 ♚c6 (It no longer matters any more whose move it is. A king and two pawns will defeat a king and none!) 20 c5 ♚c7 (or obviously 20...♚b5 21 ♚d5) 21 ♚c4. Black could draw if there were no b-pawns but they've always been in existence and White knew that eventually this day would come, i.e. Black can resign!

Sure there were other first moves possible and of course there would be transpositions. However, as I've deemed that the above constituted Black's best defence, it must be 5 points for **E**.

157

Quick View Answers

Test One

1	C	D1	
2	B		
3	E		
4	B		
5	A		
6	A		
7	D		
8	E	C2	D2
9	B	A1	C1
10	C		
11	B		
12	D		
13	C		
14	B	D1	
15	A	C1	
16	A		
17	B	C1	
18	D	A1	
19	E	C1	D1
20	C		

Test Two

1	E			
2	C	D3		
3	B			
4	D	C1		
5	E	B1	C1	D1
6	C	E3		
7	B	E2		
8	A			
9	A			
10	D	A2		
11	D	A2		
12	C			
13	B			
14	A			
15	E			
16	C	D2	E3	
17	B	C2		
18	D			
19	C	A1	B1	
20	A			

Test Three

1	D		
2	C		
3	D	E1	C1
4	B	C1	D1
5	E	C1	
6	A		
7	B	D2	
8	B		
9	B	E1	
10	E		
11	C	D2	E2
12	A		
13	C	D1	
14	D	C2	
15	E		
16	C	A2	B2
17	A		
18	B		
19	E		
20	E	B1	

Test Four

1	C	A3		
2	B	A1		
3	C			
4	D			
5	C	A2		
6	D	E1		
7	E	B2		
8	D	A2	B2	C2
9	A			
10	E			
11	B			
12	D	B2		
13	A			
14	D	A2		
15	E	B1		
16	C			
17	C			
18	D			
19	A			
20	E			

Marking Scheme

You will observe how 1 point equates to 1% and once you've totted up your score in any given test, feel free to compare your result with the figures given below. However, I must warn you not to pay too much heed to your assessment as accuracy is not guaranteed! Indeed I neither want you throwing away your chess books nor giving up your day job!

0-20% Very tricky questions. Okay, statistically speaking you may have done better by guessing without looking at the questions but of course you could easily have been put off the scent by some of my teasers. Better luck next time!

21-40% Being honest (as I always am!) you still have a fair way to improve but I suspect that it's not beyond you. Keep working at your chess and things will look rosier.

41-60% You know what it's about but now is not the time to be resting on your laurels. A reasonable score but I'm sure you could do better.

61-80% Unless you cheated, you've done pretty well. I would say that you are a strong club player with plenty of potential.

81-100% Now we're talking! Being in this very impressive score group bodes well and should be a springboard for greater success. Closer to the maximum point count and those IM or GM norms are either already in the bag or are likely to be on their way.

I hope that you are satisfied with your results and, having now read the solutions, at least understand why you may have got questions wrong. It was my primary aim to be informative and if you had fun along the way, then all the better!

Until *Chess Choice Challenge 3*, goodbye and good luck!

Chris